THE
BLOODIED
AND THE
BROKEN

THE BLOODIED
AND THE
BROKEN

Denise Noe

Black Lyon Publishing, LLC

THE BLOODIED AND THE BROKEN
TRUE TALES OF THE VICIOUS AND VICTIMIZED

This is a work of non-fiction. All direct quotes are either from
recorded interviews, interviews with individuals by local
media at the time or the recollection of the individuals during
interviews with the author of what was said at the time. When
possible, those interviewed reviewed their recollected quotes for
accuracy.

Our books may be ordered through your local bookstore or by
visiting the publisher:

www.BlackLyonPublishing.com

Black Lyon Publishing, LLC
PO Box 567
Baker City, OR 97814

ISBN: 978-1-934912-97-3
Library of Congress Control Number: 2021941582

Published and printed in the United States of America.

Black Lyon True Crime

Dedication

*To Dan Barry for being a friend
and an understanding employer.*

CONTENTS

INTRODUCTION

The articles in this collection may at first blush seem to have little in common. They include stories about crimes against strangers and intimates, children and adults. Attackers and victims vary as to time period, location, class, race/ethnicity, and gender. This volume contains stories about multiple murderers and murderers with a single victim. Two stories featured, the Barbara Payton tragedy and the David Rothenberg burning, do not revolve around murder at all but physical attacks that had devastating results.

So why did this writer select these particular cases for this collection? I chose these incidents for this collection because in all cases the victims have, at least in my opinion, a special claim on our sympathy. To put it quite simply, these are stories that revolve around an extraordinary amount of suffering. That suffering is both physical and psychological. In addition, I chose the cases I did because I believe they possess larger implications for society as a whole. These are cases that raise important, and basic, questions about cruelty and caring, about the nature of vulnerability and victimhood. They raise questions about the social ecology, as well as the possible biological factors, that lead to violent crimes. These stories focus on incidents that often throw into sharp relief the sad truth that yesterday's victim all-too-often becomes today's victimizer.

I chose to lead off with the Sylvia Likens case because it may well be the worst crime ever committed against a single victim. There are several factors that give it this hideous distinction. One is the sheer volume of physical abuse against this teenaged girl who was repeatedly beaten, kicked, burned, deprived of food and water, deprived of cleanliness, and forced to ingest waste matter. Another is the way physical abuse was fused with emotional abuse, with constant verbal attacks on her as a person, the two forms of abuse culminating in Sylvia's body being forcibly branded with stigmatizing words. Along with its "worst crime" distinction, the Likens case fascinates because it raises larger issues such as the role of poverty in creating the frustrations that lead to violent crime and the need for governmental mechanisms to protect children from abuse. The case is also significant for the "group endeavor" aspect of the case and the way in which so many people—the majority themselves children—turned so viciously on a child.

Although unusual and unusually heart-wrenching, the Sylvia Likens case may not be unique in its horror. Indeed, I included the story of 18th century midwife Elizabeth Brownrigg's beating and torturing to death of young Mary Clifford because the Likens case echoes it in several points even though the crimes took place in different countries and were separated by two centuries. There is also a link between the cases of Sylvia Likens and Mary Clifford and the more contemporary killing of Jonathan James in that all three children were brutally punished for wetting their beds. That three fatal cases of child abuse are linked to nocturnal urinary incontinence brings up myths about bedwetting as well as questions about how people view bedwetting. Of course, most punishments for bedwetting do not—thankfully—lead to a child's death.

However, the entire practice of punishing a child—or anyone—for a medical problem is appalling and appallingly common. A study done in 2014 found that about a third of bedwetting youngsters were punished for their bedwetting, a practice that did not decrease their bedwetting but contributed to depression and other psychological problems. The late actor Michael Landon, most famous for his roles in the TV shows *Bonanza, Little House on the Prairie,* and *Highway To Heaven,* bravely went public with the story of his childhood bedwetting and the cruel punishment he endured for it. During Landon's bedwetting years, his mother forced him to hang out each morning the bedsheet he had urinated on the previous night so the whole neighborhood would know he wet the bed. He used these experiences as the basis for an extraordinary 1976 made-for-TV movie called *The Loneliest Runner* about a hero who becomes a world-class runner because he races home after school each day to pull the urine-stained sheet down from his window so his classmates will not learn about his bedwetting. The truth about bedwetting is that it is not caused by laziness but is a medical problem, not subject to conscious control, and therefore an inappropriate reason for any kind of punishment.

Several cases in this volume highlight the aforementioned truth that the victimized frequently turn victimizers. "Honeymoon Killers" Raymond Fernandez and Martha Beck grew up ostracized and unfairly persecuted, Raymond because he was frail and could not measure up to his father's expectations, Martha because a glandular disorder caused extreme weight gain. They were pitiful people who turned their own hostilities against the pitifully lonely and lovelorn (and a child of an adult victim).

There are two cases in this book of parents who turned their inner turmoil and pain into terrible crimes against their own offspring. "Weak woman" Fumiko Kimura is an especially sad example of how failure and ineffectuality can lead to the most heartbreaking destruction. A seemingly loving mother, but a person unable to cope with the hand life dealt her, she brutally killed her own two very young children.

Charles Rothenberg, raised to a large extent by orphanages, never knew or experienced true love during his formative years so he grew into a warped man who mistook a sense of possession for parental love. That possessiveness led him to commit a horrible crime against the son he claimed to love, a crime that left David Rothenberg physically and emotionally scarred for life. Perhaps no case is more emblematic of the victimized-turning-victimizer than the terrifying story of Ricky "Davidito" Rodriguez. Sexually abused as a child because of the bizarre beliefs of the "Children of God" religious denomination in which he was raised, Rodriguez grew up to viciously murder one of his abusers before ending his own life.

Part of the reason I bookended the articles in this collection with the Sylvia Likens and the David Rothenberg incidents is that they are parallel in the extraordinary amount of agony endured by the victims. While Sylvia was the victim of repeated assaults over a lengthy time period, David was victimized only once but the nature of that victimization led to a lifetime of physical pain and disfigurement along with the psychology agony that resulted from his disfigurement.

Few life stories are as wrenchingly sad as that of the tragic Barbara Payton. Her beauty and acting talent took her to the pinnacle of Hollywood glamour and fame. But her beauty was the ultimate two-edged sword as it also led Payton to become the apex in a love triangle that ended with the brutal pummeling of A-list actor Franchot Tone by B-lister Tom Neal. That fistfight resulted in the collapse of Payton's once promising career in the glare of poisonous publicity. The woman who catapulted to fame and wealth in just a few years ended her life barely scraping by in a series of skid row rat-traps where she drank continuously and sold her sexual favors for a pittance.

Perhaps what most ties the cases recounted in this collection together is symbolized by its title. In many cases, a "broken" human being will "break" another, leading to a kind of cycle of brokenness. Whether victim or victimizer or victim-turned-victimizer, principal figures in the stories of this collection are indeed *The Bloodied and the Broken*.

CHAPTER 1

The Torturing to Death of Sylvia Likens

On October 26, 1965, Indianapolis police answered a call saying that a girl had died. The call came from a pay telephone in front of a Shell station in a poor section of the city. The caller was a teenaged boy whose voice had not finished changing into that of an adult man. He sounded very nervous, and directed the police to the address, 3850 East New York Street, at which they would find the dead female.

When the cops got to the dingy, rundown, clapboard home to which the anonymous caller had directed them, they found the emaciated dead body of 16-year-old Sylvia Marie Likens. She was covered with bruises and small wounds, later revealed to be cigarette and match burns that numbered over 100. There were also large areas of her body where the outer layer of skin had peeled off. Likens also had a big letter "3" branded on her chest. However, the most remarkable injuries, by far, were the words in block letters that had been burned directly onto her stomach: I'M A PROSTITUTE AND PROUD OF IT!

Thus ended one of the most horrible crimes ever committed against a single victim.

The crime had been perpetrated by an informal group of teenagers and children, some as young as 11 and 12, led by a 37-year-old woman. That woman's name was Gertrude Baniszewski (pronounced "Ban-i-SHEF-ski" rather than the more fittingly ominously sounding way it looks like it should be said: "Ban-i-ZOO-ski"). Sylvia and her younger sister, the 15-year-old disabled Jenny Fay Likens (she had a limp due to polio and a brace around that leg) had been boarding with Baniszewski since early July.

At that time, the Likens parents had left Sylvia and Jenny in the care of Mrs. Baniszewski—they knew her as "Mrs. Wright"—so they would be free to travel the carnival circuit operating a concession stand.

Baniszewski's Background

Gertrude Baniszewski's life up until the time she met the Likens family had been difficult and sad but in no way criminal (at least on her part). She was born Gertrude Van Fossan in 1929, the third of six children in a lower-class family. She always liked her dad better than her mom and suffered the trauma of watching her beloved father die of a heart attack when she was only eleven years old. Sometimes clashing with her mother as a teenager, she dropped out of high school when she was sixteen to marry 18-year-old John Baniszewski—and seems to have lived pregnantly ever after. Although John Baniszewski was a police officer, charged with enforcing the law, he frequently broke it to assault his wife when she annoyed him. John often ended disagreements between himself and Gertrude with his fists. The couple split up after a decade.

A while after she was divorced, Gertrude met and married Edward Guthrie, but the marriage lasted only three months because Edward did not want the responsibility of caring for children who were not his (at that time, Gertrude had four kids). She and John remarried each other, then divorced seven years and two more kids later in 1963. A much younger man named Dennis Lee Wright took an interest in Gertrude. He was 23 and she 37 when their romance blossomed. Although it was unfashionable at the time, they lived together briefly out of wedlock. Dennis could be abusive to his live-in girlfriend. He impregnated Gertrude twice. She suffered a miscarriage, then gave birth to Dennis, Jr. before her boyfriend absconded.

At the time of her fateful meeting with the Likens family, the underweight Baniszewski had a kind of "young-old" look about her. She had a sadly careworn and prematurely lined face. Although not yet 40 years old, she had been pregnant no less than thirteen times, giving birth seven times and enduring six miscarriages. A chain smoker, she suffered from asthma, bronchitis, and nervous tension. Her income consisted of haphazard child support payments (both of the fathers of her children were seriously delinquent) and the few dollars she managed to scrape together from occasional work like ironing and baby-sitting. Not wanting people to know that her youngest child was "illegitimate," she called herself and was called by others, "Mrs. Wright."

Betty Likens, together with daughters Sylvia and Jenny, had recently moved into one of the many rundown, boxlike little houses in the neighborhood. Betty and Lester Likens were recently separated. The family moved often as their father searched for jobs to keep the family's financial head above water. They had previously resided in this very area.

Sylvia and Jenny, together with a new friend named Darlene McGuire, were walking around the sidewalks in a normal, aimless teenaged manner when they met up with a girl named Paula Baniszewski. Paula was an overweight 17-year-old with a decided mean streak. Although not yet showing, she was also pregnant as the result of brief fling with an adult, married man.

The bunch of teenagers headed to the Baniszewski house where they shared soft drinks and laughs. Paula invited them to spend the night. Sylvia and Jenny didn't have to ask their mom for permission since she was in jail.

The next day, Lester Likens, having been informed of his wife's arrest, went with his oldest son, 19-year-old Danny, to his estranged wife's place to pick up Sylvia and Jenny. Not finding his daughters there, he began canvassing the neighborhood. Darlene MacGuire told him they were at the Baniszewskis.

When Lester got to "Mrs. Wright's" home, it was late in the evening and he was both tired and distraught. He talked about how he and Betty had reconciled and were going to travel with a carnival. Mrs. Wright graciously offered to let him spend the night sleeping on the couch in her cluttered and dusty living room.

The next day, Lester asked, or Gertrude offered (accounts are unclear), to board Sylvia and Jenny. Regardless of whose idea it was for Mrs. Wright to care for them, an agreement was made that she would board them for $20 a week.

Over a year later, in court, Lester Likens would be asked if he had inspected the home in which he left two of his five children. He replied, "I didn't pry" — an odd way to describe not bothering to take a look-see about a place one's children would be living in. If he had, he would have found that the household had no stove, only a hot plate, that it possessed fewer beds than were needed for those already living there, and that its kitchen drawers boasted a grand total of three spoons. During Sylvia's tragic stay, the pitiful number of spoons would shrink to only one.

Thus, Lester Likens placed his minor daughters in the care of a woman he had known for only a couple of days and who had not been recommended to him by anyone. He did know, however, that she had the responsibility of caring for a large family without the help of a husband or other adult in the home.

Before leaving, Lester gave Mrs. Wright some advice that he would later have much reason to regret: "You'll have to take care of these girls with a firm hand because their mother has let them do as they please."

Who was Sylvia Likens?

Sylvia's photograph shows a pretty, freckled teenager with wavy dark hair and bangs, gazing into the distance with an expression that, as one of the prosecutors said at the trial of her killers, seems "full of hope and anticipation." The girl described in *The Indiana Torture Slaying* by John Dean — he has since changed his name to Natty Bumppo to prevent confusion with the John Dean of Watergate fame—and in the non-fictional and non-speculative passages of Kate Millett's *The Basement*, appears to have been a fairly average youngster. She enjoyed attending church and made average grades in school. She liked roller skating and dancing. Nicknamed "Cookie," she is said to have had a lively sense of humor and tended to smile with her mouth closed because she was self-conscious that a front tooth was missing (the result of some childhood roughhousing with a brother).

Dean quotes an acquaintance as remembering that Sylvia felt like "the odd one in the family because she was born between two sets of twins." Both twins in the Likens family were fraternal rather than identical and both were of different sexes. Danny and Diana were two years older than Sylvia while Jenny and Benny were a year younger.

The Likens family was always poor and the marriage was troubled; Lester and Betty had split up, then gotten back together, more than once. Given the demands of two sets of twins and the extra care that had to be given Jenny because of her disability, it seems reasonable that Sylvia may have felt rather neglected by her parents.

In her 16 years of life, Sylvia had known no less than 14 addresses because the family moved so frequently. In the past, she had been left at a grandmother's house or boarded out when Lester and Betty did not find it feasible to take Sylvia and Jenny along with them.

Like most teenagers, Sylvia made a little cash through odd jobs. She baby-sat and did ironing (ironically, the same jobs Gertrude Baniszewski held). Also like most in her age group, Sylvia enjoyed music. Her favorite rock group was, unsurprisingly in that era, The Beatles. She also enjoyed singing herself. During her early time with the family B, she would sing to Stephanie Baniszewski, who returned the favor. Sylvia's favorite tune had a lyric about "all the stars in the sky."

Sylvia appears to have been very close to her disabled sister. When the girls went on one of their frequent roller skating expeditions, Jenny would put a skate on her good foot and Sylvia would pull Jenny around the ring so Jenny could experience skating even with the steel brace around one leg.

The Likens girls' first week with the Baniszewskis passed without incident, getting to know the other kids and starting at a new school. However, during the second week, the Likens parents' payment was slow to arrive. Gertrude screamed at her boarders, "I took care of you two bitches for nothing!"

Both girls had to lie across a bed and expose their bare buttocks so Baniszewski could spank them.

The payment came the next day.

However, the next week brought another paddling for the sisters because Mrs. Wright believed that Sylvia was leading the other kids into stealing out of stores.

Three major accusations against Sylvia would recur. One of them was that she was dishonest, another was that she was physically unclean, and the third, leading to the gruesome work on her belly, was that she was sexually promiscuous.

Were any of these accusations true? Sylvia's mother had shoplifted from a store in Indianapolis and Sylvia herself was to admit that she stole at least one acquisition. However, it is also true that Mrs. Wright accused the girl of stealing, and punished her for it, when she did not. The Likens family had a custom of going through debris looking for empty soda pop bottles to turn in for refunds and Gertrude would erroneously believe that treats Sylvia acquired through this means were stolen.

There is no reason—prior to her enforced dirtiness—to think that Sylvia's hygiene was particularly bad.

Sylvia was, in all likelihood, a virgin. It is also possible that she was flirtatious.

Gertrude Baniszewski was probably projecting her personal fears outward through these charges. There is no evidence that she ever stole but theft had to be sorely tempting to one in her circumstances. Her personal hygiene and the cleanliness of her household were poor, which is understandable considering that she was a chronically ill woman trying to cope with many youngsters and an infant. She had reason to fear for her own and her daughters' reputations for chastity since she had twice been pregnant out of wedlock and, at the time the Likens girls stayed in her house, her own 17-year-old unmarried daughter Paula was pregnant.

Early in her stay, Sylvia attended church each Sunday with the Baniszewski kids. Paula Baniszewski tattled to her mother that Sylvia had pigged out at a church supper so Mrs. Wright and some of the children came up with a punishment that had, as many of the torments inflicted on the Likens girl would, a perverse logic to it. Sylvia's frankfurter was passed around the Baniszewski table and loaded with condiments. Sylvia was ordered to eat this concoction. The girl complied, then promptly vomited—and was forced to eat her vomit.

Sometime after this, Mr. and Mrs. Likens stopped by for a visit, as they had a few days after their daughters had been paddled for the late payment. On this occasion, as on the previous visit and those that would follow, neither of the Likens girls complained about the way they were being treated.

"Was she a Masochist?"

This leads us to a troubling psychological puzzle. In his foreword to *The Indiana Torture Slaying*, prosecutor Leroy K. New says, "I have been repeatedly asked why Sylvia did not just simply run away." When the crime was first discovered, a newspaper reporter asked, "Was she a masochist?"

There are several things, other than masochism, which could account for her passivity. First, Sylvia had a limited frame of reference as to what constitutes inappropriate discipline. As noted by Dean, Sylvia and Jenny "were accustomed to being punished, often unjustly." The early "paddlings" the Likens girls received might have been unfair but were not clearly abusive. Grown-ups frequently make issues out of youngsters' eating habits as in the universally famous "eat your vegetables!" scolding so even the hotdog with way-too-much of "everything on it" would not necessarily be seen as beyond the pale, especially by children whose frame of reference is necessarily limited.

What's more, at least one adult witnessed abusive incidents and, although disturbed by them, did not consider them serious enough to report them to the police.

According to *The Indiana Torture Slaying,* a middle-aged couple with two kids, Raymond and Phyllis Vermillion, moved next door to the Baniszewskis late in August 1965. Phyllis Vermillion worked the night shift at an RCA plant and needed a baby-sitter for her children. She decided to visit Gertrude Baniszewski, thinking that the mother of seven who had taken in two boarders might be a good person to care for the Vermillion youngsters.

The two neighbors sat around a table and drank coffee while kids yelled at each other and baby Dennis fussed and cried. Vermillion noticed a slim, pretty but timid and nervous-looking girl who had a black eye. "That's Sylvia," sighed Gertrude. Paula Baniszewski added, "I gave her the black eye." Just before making this boast, however, Paula filled a glass with hot water and threw it at Sylvia.

Understandably, Phyllis Vermillion decided to look elsewhere for a baby-sitter. Less understandably, she did not report what she had seen and heard to the authorities. Then again, standards of discipline were wider in the time period than they are today so she simply may not have thought of it as "abuse," much less a crime.

Early in October, Vermillion paid another social call to the large family next door. Again she saw Sylvia, who looked dazed, even zombified, and who again had a black eye. This time, the teenager also had a swollen lip. "I beat her up," Paula readily volunteered. Later, Paula began hitting the listless girl with a belt.

Once again Phyllis Vermillion left the house without believing she had seen something the police ought to know about. If a supposedly normal, responsible adult could not recognize these actions as criminal, how can anyone expect an untutored teenager like Sylvia to be able to do so?

Running away may never have occurred to her. Where would she go? Additionally, by the time sleeping out in the street became preferable to life with the Baniszewskis, it was no longer an option: she was tied up and/or locked in the cellar.

In fact, there was one instance, which will be described later in this essay, in which she and Jenny did complain about mistreatment. They were not believed. The fear of being disbelieved—which would prove well founded—probably contributed to Sylvia's previous silence.

Another reason for her failure to complain about the mistreatment may be that she anticipated the question traditionally asked of kids who get picked—Why don't other people like you?—and knew she could not answer it

Complaining to others would have meant having to tell them what had been done to her. As the mistreatment worsened, it is likely that shame silenced Sylvia.

Both Sylvia and her sister were, for good reason, terrified of Gertrude. They greatly feared the woman's wrath if they should "tell," anticipating that, instead of being rescued, they would incur still more punishment/abuse.

Finally, Sylvia was probably fiercely protective of her disabled younger sister and feared that "telling" would lead to revenge being taken out on Jenny.

The Slow Slide into Horror

It is important to emphasize the truth that Sylvia's life at the Baniszewskis did not turn into a horror overnight. It was a slow slide from getting unfairly punished on occasion in July, to getting "picked on" and physically hurt in various ways regularly around August and September, to the mind-boggling torture that characterized the last few weeks of Sylvia's brief life in October.

During her first weeks with Gertrude, Sylvia went to the same church the Baniszewskis did, listened to phonograph records with the other kids, watched TV, and took trips to the park with friends. She attended high school with Stephanie and Paula. She ate with Gertrude and the other kids.

Of course, meals at the Baniszewski home were not a terribly enjoyable experience for any of its residents. Ten people had to be fed without a stove. They ate things like crackers and sandwiches. Soup formed a major part of their diets since it could be heated up on the hot plate. However, they had to eat it in shifts since they had just three spoons when Sylvia got there, then two, and finally only one. The sole spoon would be used, rinsed off in the sink, and then handed to the next hungry person.

It is believed that, sometime late in August, Sylvia let it slip that she had once allowed a boyfriend to get under the bed covers with her. Gertrude was outraged. "You're going to have a baby!" Gertrude announced. Then Mrs. Wright kicked the girl hard in the crotch. Many more kicks to the genitals would follow and the autopsy would show that Sylvia's pubic area was horribly mauled and swollen.

Sylvia's imagined pregnancy also outraged the genuinely pregnant Paula Baniszewski. Seeing Sylvia seated, Paula knocked Sylvia onto the floor, saying, "You ain't fit to sit in a chair."

Apparently as revenge, Sylvia told some of her fellow students at Tech High School that the two oldest Baniszewski girls, Stephanie and Paula, were "prostitutes."

Stephanie's 15-year-old boyfriend, Coy Hubbard, heard about the planting of this defamatory and false accusation against his ladylove, flew into a rage, and beat Sylvia up. Coy was a handsome guy with dark, curly hair. He was big for his age and frequently a disciplinary problem at school. As he would many times in the future, Coy practiced judo on Sylvia, flipping her against walls and onto the floor. Mrs. Wright gave Sylvia yet another paddling.

Mrs. Wright encouraged neighborhood children to believe bad things about Sylvia and take "revenge." Heavyset, 13-year-old Anna Siscoe liked Sylvia—until Gertrude told Anna that Sylvia had said Anna's mother was a prostitute. Anna viciously attacked the older girl. During the melee, Sylvia is reported to have clutched her stomach, saying "Oh, my baby!"

It appears that Sylvia, although probably a virgin, had been convinced by those around her that she really must be pregnant. She may have been ignorant of the specifics of reproduction.

Gertrude whispered similar things about Sylvia making sexually-oriented slanders into the ears of her daughter Paula as well as a girl named Judy Duke and more fights resulted with Sylvia left bruised and bloodied.

Was Sylvia impugning the morals of the females around her? It is possible. She was being taunted about her own alleged sexual indiscretions and may have tried to direct similar negative attention elsewhere to take it off of herself. *You're weird. No, you are,* are dueling insults heard each day on schoolyards throughout the world. However, it's also possible that Gertrude was making false accusations to get others stirred up against her favorite scapegoat.

Paula Baniszewski soon made a hobby out of plunking Sylvia in the head with anything that came to hand whether dish, bottle, or can. Often when a group was tormenting Sylvia, her sister Jenny would be ordered to hit her. Timidly, Jenny refused. An infuriated Gertrude slapped her face. Jenny then complied but later said she used her left hand instead of her right (she is right-handed) so it would not really hurt Sylvia.

The Sexless Sex Crime

In early October, an incident occurred that led Mrs. Wright to order Sylvia to quit school. Sylvia had no gym suit for her physical education class and Gertrude would not give her the money to buy one. However, Sylvia came home from school with just such a suit that she claimed she had "found." Gertrude believed, not unreasonably, that the suit was a theft. Badgered about it, Sylvia confessed that she had indeed stolen it. The woman slapped and kicked the girl, then whipped her with a belt.

Mrs. Wright left the subject of Sylvia's stealing to return to that of her alleged promiscuity and, after scolding the teenager, began kicking her in the crotch area. Later that day, still not satisfied that the girl had been adequately punished for theft, she applied a lighted match to Sylvia's "sticky fingers" and gave her yet another whipping.

Heat would become a major feature of Sylvia's torture. Its origin probably lies in an incident in which Gertrude Baniszewski's abusive boyfriend, Dennis Wright, put a cigarette out on her neck.

The motley group began burning Sylvia with cigarettes and lighted matches. Paula Baniszewski broke her hand hitting Sylvia, then used the cast to beat the girl. The favorite pastime of several kids in the area was getting Sylvia: kicking, hitting, flipping her around through Coy Hubbard's judo tricks or imitations of them, and burning her.

The autopsy would disclose two indices of how much agony Sylvia would endure: she had broken each of her fingernails backward in painful clawing and had bitten her lower lip so deeply it was partially severed.

As the persecution of Sylvia worsened, it became increasingly sexual in character. However, it was also a peculiarly "sexless sex crime." The sexual aspect started with the constant teasing, alleging that she was sexually promiscuous and escalated with Mrs. Wright's vicious kicks to the girl's crotch.

There would be other sexual-like assaults, including one to be described shortly, but no "sexual assaults" in the standard meaning of the term. There are no reports of Gertrude ever touching Sylvia in any manner suggestive of lesbianism. None of the young males who excitedly took part in the beating and torturing of the girl are believed to have either raped her vaginally, orally, or anally. The autopsy would disclose a gross swelling of Likens' genital region due to the kicks. However, the autopsy found none of the internal vaginal lacerations consistent with rape and tests for semen were be negative.

Since the group inflicted almost every sort of assault the human mind could come up with, the omission is puzzling. Mrs. Wright probably had a horror of being thought "perverted" (assuming she was even familiar with the term) which would explain her not assaulting her victim's sex organ with fingers or tongue. Perhaps Coy Hubbard feared offending Stephanie if his girlfriend considered a rape "two-timing." It is also possible, as Millett speculates in some of her more credible fictional passages in *The Basement: Meditations on a Human Sacrifice*, that they genuinely believed Sylvia was a "slut" and feared sexually transmitted diseases or a more ambiguous sort of "contamination" from such contact.

On one awful day, Mrs. Wright was indignant because she was told that, much earlier in the girl's stay, Sylvia had had a bit of extra cash. She knew that the girl had to have been either stealing or prostituting. Sylvia could not just be turning in empty soda pop bottles as she said. So, while several kids were at the Baniszewski house, Gertrude forced Sylvia to perform an awkward striptease in front of the gloating group. When Sylvia was fully nude, Mrs. Wright made the weeping girl shove a soft drink bottle up her vagina.

One night in October, Sylvia wet her bed. This could have been the result of psychological anxiety—if anyone ever had reason to be nervous, she did—or it could have been because the many cruel blows to her stomach and crotch had weakened control in that area. However, her tormentors decided that she must now live down in the basement with the dog because she was too dirty to live with human beings. She was also prevented from using the toilet and, thus, forced her to repeatedly befoul herself.

At the same time, her torturers began a regimen of forced bathing in which they tied up the "dirty girl" and shoved her into the Baniszewski's old-fashioned, claw-footed bathtub tub after filling it with scalding hot water. Sometimes she was put in the tub by Gertrude and Paula and on some evenings 14-year-old Richard (Ricky) Hobbs was there to assist. Hobbs was a soft-featured, good-looking lad who sported straight blonde hair parted on the side, wore thick spectacles with black horn rims and often hung out at the Baniszewski house.

Paula Baniszewski rubbed salt into Sylvia's wounds.

Sylvia was often kept nude or nearly so for days at a time. She became a game for the neighborhood kids to enjoy, burning, punching, and sometimes pushing her down the stairs to the cellar, then forcing her back up just to throw her back down again.

On one occasion, the starving teenager was allowed up from the cellar and told to try to eat soup with her fingers. Famished, she made an attempt at it only to have the soup grabbed away from her by John. Later, Mrs. Wright and John forced the girl to eat shit and drink urine.

No Rescue

One of the most depressing aspects of the Sylvia Likens case is the realization that there were several times when, if people had acted just a bit differently than they did, Sylvia could have been rescued. People have always asked, "Why didn't they tell someone?" In September, Sylvia and Jenny told someone. That someone was their older, married sister, Diana Shoemaker, a slim, attractive woman with jet black hair. Sylvia was being picked on, both girls said. Every time something, anything, went wrong, Mrs. Wright would shout, "Paula, get the board!" Jenny backed up Sylvia's claim that the latter was constantly punished for things she didn't do.

Diana blew them off. They were exaggerating. They had to be. No one likes to be punished but they probably deserved it, she thought.

The Baniszewski home had visitors. Phyllis Vermillion's visits, the assaults she witnessed, and her failure to do anything about them have already been described.

A 12-year-old girl named Judy Duke described some of the goings-on she had witnessed in the Baniszewski home to her mother while Mrs. Duke was washing dishes. "They were beating and kicking Sylvia something terrible!" the girl reported.

"Oh, well, they're just punishing her, aren't they?" Mrs. Duke asked rhetorically.

The Rev. Roy Julian tried to visit all the members of his congregation. The Baniszewskis attended his fundamentalist Christian church and he was at their home in September. He and Mrs. Wright chatted amiably while sitting on the worn living room couch. Mrs. Wright complained about her husband's failure to pay child support, her numerous medical problems, and all the troubles she had with the kids. Sylvia was by far the worst of the lot, Mrs. Wright asserted. In a horrified tone, she told the man of God, "Sylvia has been skipping school and making advances on older men—for money!"

Rev. Julian remembered Sylvia, the pretty girl who had "come forward" one Sunday at his church to profess her Christian faith. How awful if she should be sinning so terribly! He asked to speak with Sylvia. Perhaps he could help the child see the error of her ways and mend them.

Gertrude told him, "Ask her sister."

Jenny, who had been constantly threatened by Mrs. Wright, mechanically recited some of Sylvia's misdeeds: "She tells lies. And at night, after all of us go to bed, she slips down and raids the icebox." Jenny hoped she could please Mrs. Wright without having to repeat the most humiliating, sexual sins attributed to her sister. It appeared to work.

Rev. Julian prayed with Gertrude, then left.

He came back for another visit a few weeks. Again Mrs. Wright complained about the terrible problems she was having with Sylvia. "Sylvia said at school that Paula is going to have a baby," Gertrude claimed. "But I know my daughter, and I know Sylvia. Paula's not going to have a baby; it's Sylvia."

The minister was concerned about the hostility Paula had confessed she harbored. "Paula told me," he said, "that there was hatred in her heart for Sylvia."

Mrs. Wright told him it was the other way around and the minister left the house for the last time.

Sometime in October, Diana Shoemaker came to the home to visit her sisters. Gertrude could not allow her to see the condition that Sylvia was in so she refused to permit Shoemaker to enter the residence. Gerty claimed the Likens parents had given her permission to keep Diana away from her sisters. Diana insisted that she wanted to see her sisters and Mrs. Wright ordered her away, threatening to have the young woman arrested for trespassing.

Very shortly before Sylvia died, Jenny ran into Diana on the street. Diana wanted to talk with Jenny but the latter told her older sister, "I can't talk to you or I'll get in trouble," and hurried away from her.

A public health agency had received a report about a girl suffering running, open sores at the Baniszewski house. Who is was who made this report remains a mystery to this day. A public health nurse came to the door October 15. She was attired in a starchy white uniform. "Mrs. Wright?" she asked.

Gertrude nodded and invited her in.

The stranger informed Gertrude that she was a public health nurse and wanted to talk about Mrs. Wright's children because of an anonymous report that there was a girl there with multiple sores.

Jenny was in the room at the time, terrified of Gertrude yet suddenly full of hope. Was this rescue?

Mrs. Wright looked at her with eyes that must have been full of menace, repeating silently the threat she so often made to the girl verbally: "If you say anything about Sylvia, you'll get the same treatment she's getting." Out loud, Gertrude ordered Jenny to go to the kitchen and do dishes. Jenny promptly complied.

Then Mrs. Wright turned her attention back to the nurse. "I know who you're looking for," she began, "Jenny's sister Sylvia. She has sores all over her body. She won't keep herself clean. I finally kicked her out of the house. She's not worthy to stay here. She's a prostitute." Gerty told the concerned nurse, "I don't know where she would be now."

The two of them were, in fact, sitting right above the basement in which Sylvia was locked and bound.

The nurse returned to her office. There she filed the report on the Baniszewskis on a "one time only" card, meaning there was to be no follow-up.

Just five days before Sylvia's death, the police came to the Baniszewski residence. Gertrude called them. As reported by John Dean/Natty Bumppo, "Robert Bruce Hanlon, banged on the door that evening, demanding the return of some things he said the children had stolen from his basement. Gertrude told him he was knocking on the wrong door … She called the police, telling them she had found Hanlon halfway through her window. The police locked him up on a burglary charge."

Phyllis and Ray Vermillion witnessed these events from their car. They were parked at the curb at the time. Phyllis Vermillion became concerned about Hanlon and talked to the police about him, helping to free him of the charge. One wonders again why she didn't tell the police, at this time or previously, about the things she had witnessed involving Sylvia.

Sylvia's Last Weekend

The last weekend of Sylvia's life began when Mrs. Wright decided to let her sleep upstairs in a bed again. However, she attached a strange condition to this: Gertrude instructed John and Coy to tie Sylvia to the bed so she could not get up during the night to go to the bathroom. "You can't go to the bathroom," Gertrude said, "until you've learned not to wet the bed." Sylvia, whose genital and urinary region had been damaged through repeated abuse, was prevented from taking a trip to the bathroom to avoid wetting the bed.

Sylvia wet the bed that night.

The next morning began with a second forced striptease, again climaxed by Gertrude forcing Sylvia to insert a soda bottle up her vagina. Then Mrs. Wright decided to take another revenge on Sylvia for having slandered Paula and Stephanie at Tech High. "You have branded my daughters so I will brand you!" she told the confused teenager.

Then Gerty suggested to Ricky Hobbs that he "tattoo" Sylvia with the words "I'm a prostitute and proud of it!" He eagerly accepted the assignment. Sylvia was forcibly stripped, then tied down and gagged. Gertrude heated a sewing needle and carved an "I," apostrophe and part of the "M" before handing the needle to Hobbs and telling him to finish the job.

Ricky started carving, then stopped to ask Mrs. Wright how to spell prostitute. She wrote the message out on a piece of paper for him and he burned it into Sylvia's belly.

In a few minutes, Ricky, Paula, and 10-year-old Shirley Baniszewski decided to put another brand on Sylvia. It would be a letter "S" for Sylvia or slave (this point is confused). Ricky burned the first curve onto Sylvia's chest. Then he and Shirley called Jenny over and ordered her to put the second burn on. Jenny was petrified. When she had tried to get out of hitting Sylvia, she had been slapped. Would she be burned if she refused to inflict this torture? Despite her terror, she refused. Shirley burned the second curve on but got it backward so that the number "3" appeared on Sylvia's chest.

In front of Randy Lepper, Shirley Baniszewski, Richard Hobbs, and Jenny Likens, Mrs. Wright taunted Sylvia about the words burned into her stomach. "What are you going to do now Sylvia?" Gertrude shouted. "You can't get married now, you can't undress in front of anyone. What are you going to do now?"

The weeping, mutilated girl choked out between sobs: "I guess there's nothing I can do. It's on there."

That evening, Sylvia was again relegated to the basement where Coy Hubbard flipped her against the walls. Later, Jenny visited her sister who told her: "I'm going to die. I can tell."

Sylvia was allowed to sleep upstairs that night and the next afternoon she was bathed by Mrs. Wright and Stephanie; however, this was a normal, warm bath rather than a scalding one.

Then Gertrude and Paula forced Sylvia to write a letter to her parents. Sylvia started to begin the note like the one she had previously been forced to write, "Dear Mom and Dad," but Mrs. Wright told her to stop and made her start over with the peculiar salutation, "To Mr. and Mrs. Likens." After Sylvia's death, this letter would be turned over to a cop by Mrs. Wright. She would tell him that Sylvia had been absent from her house for a few days, then wandered into the backyard, clutching this epistle. The unsigned note read, in part, as follows.

To Mr. and Mrs. Likens:
I went with a gang of boys in the middle of the night. And they said that they would pay me if I would give them something so I got in the car and they all got what they wanted … and when they got finished they beat me up and left sores on my face and all over my

body.

And they also put on my stomach, I am a prostitute and proud of it.

I have done just about everything that I could do just to make Gertie mad and cause [sic] Gertie more money than she's got. I've tore up a new mattress and peaed [sic] on it. I have also cost Gertie doctor bills that she really can't pay and made Gertie a nervous wreck and all her kids.

Mrs. Wright discussed having someone drop Sylvia in a waste lot. She told John and Jenny that they were going to do this chore that but, before they could, Sylvia made an escape attempt. The hideously mutilated and weakened girl raced to the front door. Gertrude ran after her, catching her just as Sylvia was about to make it to the porch. Then Mrs. Wright dragged her to the kitchen and offered the girl some toast. The sick youngster said she could not swallow. Infuriated, Mrs. Wright beat her across the mouth with a curtain rod.

Twelve-year-old John Baniszewski tied Sylvia up in the basement. Apparently, not wanting her young charge to die—at least not until she was elsewhere—Gertrude went down to the basement with an offer of crackers.

"Give it to the dog," Sylvia told her captor, "It's hungrier than I am." Perhaps Sylvia felt she had nothing left to lose and, so, was defiant. Or perhaps the horror of the words branded upon her had sapped her will to live. Mrs. Wright repeatedly punched the girl in the stomach.

The next day was Sunday, October 24. Gertrude and John both beat the girl. Mrs. Wright swung at Sylvia with a chair but it broke before it hit her. The frazzled woman then tried to hit Sylvia with the paddle but hit herself instead, blackening her own eye. Then Coy Hubbard stopped by and hit Sylvia in the head with a broomstick, knocking her unconscious.

During the night, Sylvia repeatedly pounded on the floor of her basement-prison with a shovel. Neighbors were disturbed and considered calling the cops to complain about the noise, but did not.

The next day, Sylvia was taken upstairs for a final—non-torturous—bath. She was placed in the tub clothed. When taken out of it, Stephanie and Ricky realized that Sylvia was not breathing. Stephanie attempted to give Sylvia mouth-to-mouth resuscitation. It did no good.

Sylvia was dead.

Mrs. Wright told Ricky to call the cops. He had to go to a pay phone since Gertrude's home did not possess a telephone. When the police got to the house, a frantic Mrs. Wright handed them the letter quoted above, hoping it would absolve her of blame for the battered corpse lying on a mattress. However, before the officer had a chance to read it, a grieving and terrified Jenny Likens whispered to him, "Get me out of here and I'll tell you everything."

Gertrude Baniszewski (authorities called her by this name upon learning she had not been legally married to Dennis Wright) was arrested for murder. So were Paula Baniszewski, Stephanie Baniszewski, John Baniszewski, Richard Hobbs, and Coy Hubbard. Younger juveniles Anna Siscoe, Judy Duke, Randy Lepper, and Mike Monroe were charged with "injury to person." Most of the youngsters readily admitted their actions but when asked for an explanation, deferred to their mother or, if unrelated, offered the excuse, "Gertie told me to."

The poverty stricken and chronically ill Mrs. Wright was hardly charismatic; she was neither hypnotist nor dominatrix but the minors apparently had faith that her "grown-up" status would protect them from the consequences of their actions. As it turned out, they would be appallingly successful in hiding behind her skirt.

The Torture Killers on Trial

The charges of injury to person were dropped against the younger juveniles. Stephanie Baniszewski's attorney got her a separate trial and later the murder charge against her was dropped as well.

Standing trial for first-degree murder in Indiana's most sensational case ever were five people: one adult, Gertrude

Baniszewski and four minors, Paula Baniszewski, John Baniszewski, Richard Hobbs, and Coy Hubbard. John had only recently turned 13.

Paula's time in court would be interrupted by a trip to the hospital to deliver the baby, even though both she and her mother had so adamantly insisted she was not pregnant. It was a girl. In a display of filial devotion, Paula named her child Gertrude.

The courtroom was jam-packed with spectators every day. This was the worst single murder the state of Indiana had ever known and the largest number of defendants it had ever tried at once. The prosecution was seeking the death penalty for all the accused and it was widely expected that, at least in Mrs. Baniszewski's case, they would get it. The death penalty in Indiana at the time was carried out by the electric chair.

Many years later, John Baniszewski was to tell a reporter that he actively enjoyed being on trial. He commented, "I took a kind of delight in it. What I really wanted was love but I took the attention instead."

The judge at the trial was Saul Rabb, a grizzled, balding, and bespectacled jurist known for his tart tongue. Representing Gertrude Baniszewski was William Erbecker, a respected, heavy-set attorney considered flamboyant and personable. George Rice, a Ph.D in psychology as well as a member of the bar, was Paula's lawyer. John's attorney, Forrest Bowman, was widely regarded as thorough and dedicated. All of these lawyers worked for their indigent clients free of charge. The only paid attorney, James G. Nedeff, had been appointed by the court to represent Richard Hobbs. Coy Hubbard was, at first represented by Joseph Quill. Quill quit after a week and Forrest Bowman assumed Hubbard's case as well as John Baniszewsi's.

The prosecution team was led by Leroy New, a tall, handsome 40-something fellow known for his skill in cross examination. Assisting him was deputy prosecutor Marjorie Wessner. Although women lawyers were still a rarity in those days, the thinking was that it was good to have a female on hand in cases involving women and child defendants and witnesses.

Much of the testimony was sensational and pathetic, often at the same time. Early witnesses included the shocked police officers who had encountered the hideously mutilated corpse of Sylvia Likens along with doctors who enumerated her extraordinary wounds. The star witness for the prosecution was Jenny Likens. She hobbled to the witness stand in a new dress and, in a voice sometimes firm, sometimes halting, and often choked with tears, detailed the horrors she and her sister had suffered.

When Wessner gently asked her why she hadn't sought help, young Likens replied, "I was scared. Gertrude just kept beating me." Defense attorneys would pursue this point at length. Jenny's response was always the same: "Gertrude threatened me if I told anyone, I'd get the same treatment Sylvia was getting."

Although tried together, the attorneys for the defendants often worked at cross-purposes. Gertrude Baniszewski's story was that she had been too sick and chronically tired to know all the terrible things going on in her own home. The children had gone wild on Sylvia without her knowledge. The attorneys for the youngsters tried to shift as much blame as possible onto Mrs. Baniszewski or the other kids.

Mrs. Baniszewski testified in her own defense. She firmly denied all the terrible acts attributed to her. She did not "strike, beat, or kick" Sylvia. Gertrude tried to "paddle" Sylvia but was too weak and had to call Paula to finish the job. She also recalled slapping a misbehaving Sylvia's hands. With all the kids in her home, both her own and their many friends, a lot of fights broke out. Mrs. Baniszewski sometimes tried to break them up, she testified, but was usually too weak and sick even to make the effort.

However, even as Gertrude testified for herself, she often seemed to be testifying against the dead Sylvia. Her story of how she first heard about Sylvia brings up the issue of the girl's sexual conduct. According to Mrs. Baniszewski's testimony, a girl came to her door looking for Darlene MacGuire, who often visited the Baniszewski kids. Mrs. B. went to the door with Darlene and the visitor "related to Darlene—she wanted to know whether she knew where she could get hold of Sylvia Likens … the reason this woman was hunting for Sylvia was suppsed to have been Sylvia had been out with her husband … Darlene brought Sylvia Likens over to our home two days later and introduced her as the girl this other girl was looking for. That is how I first became acquainted with Sylvia Likens."

Another way the accused appeared to attempt to indict the victim occured in her description of how the agreement to board the two girls was made. "Sylvia asked her father if she could stay with us," Mrs. B. claimed. "… I immediately said, 'No, I could not take care of you children. I have too many of my own and too many worries and too many responsibilities without adding any more. [Sylvia] said, 'Well, we can take care of ourselves, we are used to that.'" Just determined to live with the Baniszewskis—at least as Gertrude told it—Sylvia "turned around to her father and said, 'Daddy, you could pay her for letting us stay here.'"

In an exchange with the prosecutor, the accused insisted that Sylvia was unremittingly rebellious.

BANISZEWSKI: She would not do anything I told her, no.

NEW: She was disobedient?

BANISZEWSKI: She would not mind me, no.

NEW: Did you whip her for that?

BANISZEWSKI: I believe I testified I whipped her. Or tried to one time.

NEW: How many times was she disobedient to you?

BANISZEWSKI: I told you she would not mind me at all.

NEW: How many times.

BANISZEWSKI: I think I answered your question. I said she would not mind at all.

NEW: Ever?

BANISZEWSKI: Not that I can recall.

To back up Mrs. B.'s story, Marie Baniszewski was called to the stand. Only 11 years-old, Marie was a lovely girl with dark blonde hair cut short and curly bangs over her forehead. She appeared in court in a blue pastel dress with eyelet sleeves. Her expression was understandably somber. Her eyes were blurred with tears as she got into the witness box. Tears streamed down her pale cheeks when Erbecker asked her why she was there. Marie replied, "I'm here to testify to see if my mom killed Sylvia Likens."

Marie testified that she had seen her mom hit Sylvia only "when she was bad." She went on to swear that she had never seen her mother kick the girl, burn her, or mistreat her in any other manner. Marie had seen other kids do all those things but her mom wasn't present; she was in bed sick.

The next day Marie was cross-examined by New. The elementary-school-aged child was tearful right from the start. Asked why by the prosecutor, she replied, believably enough, "I'm nervous!"

Marie repeated the denials of the previous day to the prosecutor, whose questions of this fragile witness were relatively low-key. Finally, he took her to the day Sylvia was branded on the stomach. As she had previously, Marie maintained that it was her 10-year-old sister Shirley who had lit the matches for the needle and that her mom was in bed sick, knowing nothing of the mutilation.

New continued questioning Marie until finally the sobbing child shouted, "Oh, God, help me!" Then, Perry Mason-like, the witness for the defense turned into one for the prosecution. Marie had heated the needle; her mother had been there and started the "tattoo." She had seen Mom burn Sylvia and beat her. She had heard her mother order Sylvia down to the basement.

In his summation to the jury, Erbecker relied on the only possible mitigating factor in Mrs. B.'s defense—mental incompetence – even though her official plea was a simple *Not Guilty.* "I condemn her for being a murderess, that's what I do," Erbecker said, "but I say she's not responsible because she's not all here!" He pointed to his head.

The other defense attorneys all tried to shove as much blame onto Gertrude and the others as possible while pleading that the tender ages of their own clients made them less than fully responsible.

Prosecutor New made an impassioned plea for the death penalty for all of the accused. He told them that, "The issue here is ... law and order. Will we allow such acts? Will we allow such brutality on a human being? ... If you go below the death penalty in this case, you will lower the value of human life by that much for each defendant."

When the verdicts, came back, only Gertrude Baniszewski was convicted of first-degree murder. To the surprise and consternation of many observers, the jury did not sentence her to death. She appealed and was granted a new trial in which she was again convicted of first-degree murder and sentenced to life in prison.

Paula was convicted of second-degree murder. She appealed and was granted a new trial but passed it up to plead guilty to voluntary manslaughter. She was released after a few years.

The murder charge against Stephanie Baniszewski was dropped as were the injury to person charges and Anna Siscoe, Judy Duke, Randy, Lepper, and Mike Monroe.

John Baniszewski, Coy Hubbard, and Richard Hobbs were convicted of manslaughter. Each spent a grand total of 18 months in a juvenile detention facility.

1985: SLAM into Action

In 1985, after serving two decades in Indiana Women's Prison, the parole board voted to grant Gertrude Baniszewski a parole. However, a court ruled that the board's hearing had not been properly open to the public and a new vote had to be taken.

Two anti-crime groups, Protect the Innocent and Society's League Against Molestation (SLAM), instantly swung into action. Interestingly, SLAM was founded by Patti Linebaugh, the grandmother of Amy Sue Seitz, a two-year-old molested, tortured, and murdered by convicted child molester Theodore Frank. Perpetrated in California, that crime, like this one, would be called "the worst crime ever committed against one victim in the state's history."

Members of SLAM and Protect the Innocent pounded the pavements of Indianapolis seeking signatures of citizens opposed to the parole. They had no trouble getting them even among those who were too young to remember the case because Gertrude Baniszewski's name had, in the two decades of her incarceration, become that of an Indianapolis "boogeywoman." They ended up gathering more than 4,500 signatures in just a couple of months. Jenny Likens appeared on television to demand that the notorious Baniszewski be kept behind bars.

Despite the outcry, when the parole board again voted, it was three to two in favor of the parole, exactly as it had been on the first vote. Baniszewski's conduct as a prisoner had been quite good. She worked in the sewing shop and tended to make favorable impressions upon both prison staff and other inmates. Many of the younger imprisoned women called the child killer and mother of seven by a title most familiar to her: "Mom." According to the *Chicago Tribune,* prison psychiatrists "termed Baniszewski a 'healthy, stable, pleasant and agreeable' person who wants 'to try to make up for the past and leave the world a little better.'"

At the hearing, Baniszewski teared up frequently and expressed remorse but claimed amnesia about the crime. Indeed, her statement of remorse was enigmatic: "I'm not sure what role I had in it … because I was on drugs. I never really knew her. [But] I take full responsibility for whatever happened to Sylvia." She left prison December 4, 1985.

The torture-murderer moved to Iowa where she lived out her life under the name Nadine Van Fossan. A long-time heavy smoker, she died in 1990 of lung cancer.

Richard Hobbs, who did most of the dirty work of etching the words into Sylvia and half that of burning the "3," died of cancer when he was only 21.

Coy Hubbard, who took such excessive revenge again and again for a slur against his ladylove, Stephanie Baniszewski, served time for burglary some years after his brief stint in the reformatory. He obtained work as a mechanic. He was later tried but acquitted for the murders of two men.

John Baniszewski surfaced a few years ago after the Jonesboro, Arkansas tragedy in which a couple of junior high schook students gunned down four peers and a teacher. He decided to come forward to say that there is hope for young murderers and that they can turn their lives around. Baniszewski had changed his name to John Blake

When he spoke publicly for the first time about Sylvia's death he said he still could not adequately explained why he and the others turned on the girl the way they did. He said that he harbored a great deal of anger over his parents' marital breakup and the lack of adequate food and clothing for him and his siblings.

Blake acknowledges that his punishment was inadequate to the terrible crime. "A more severe punishment would have been just," he comments. Blake claims he turned his life around after finding God. However, the Baniszewski family went to a fundamentalist church both before and during the time the unfortunate Likens girls boarded with them. In his adult life, Blake has had no run-ins with the law. He has worked as a truck driver and realtor and served as a lay pastor. He is happily married and the father of three although he is now disabled by diabetes. His vision is blurred and he requires the assistance of a cane or walker to get around.

Stephanie Baniszewski became a schoolteacher. She also married and had kids as did Paula who moved to Iowa and is said to live on a small farm there. It is not known whether or not she had contact with her paroled mother.

The Likens family continued to endure considerable hardship. Jenny Likens enrolled in a Job Corps program in 1966 and later got a job in a bank. She also married. Lester and Betty divorced in 1967. Benny Likens, Jenny's twin brother began showing signs of severe mental illness a few years after his sister's hideous death. He became a semi-recluse, tormented by voices only he could hear.

Betty Likens died in 1999 at the age of 71. A search of her keepsakes revealed a yellowed newspaper clipping of Gertrude Baniszewski's obituary together with a note by Jenny saying, "Some good news. Damn old Gertrude died. Ha ha ha! I am happy about that."

Benny Likens died only four months after his mother. He was 49 and had been mentally troubled for some time. Only fifteen when his sister Sylvia died, he served in the army and worked in various restaurants, often as a cook, when he got out. He started hearing voices and was diagnosed as a schizophrenic. According to the afterward in *The Indiana Torture Slaying,* Lester Likens found out his son was dead when a letter the father had written to Benny was returned marked, "Deceased."

The people of Indianapolis have not forgotten Sylvia. A memorial to her will be dedicated this year on June 22. A poem by Ivan Rogers will be on the plaque, reading: "I see a light; hope. I feel a breeze; strength. I hear a song; relief. Let them through for they are the welcome ones."

Inspired by the Likens Case

The murder of Sylvia Likens has been dealt with in at least five, and possibly six, works. The easiest to get hold of is *The Basement* by feminist Kate Millett. Prior to starting this book, Millett had put on several sculptural exhibitions inspired by the Likens case.

The Basement is an odd combination of nonsense and brilliance, of fact and fiction together with the author's personal reactions to the crime. Millett reads all kinds of cosmic implications into it and projects her own beliefs—pacifist as much as feminist—onto the dead girl in ways that defy credibility.

On the other hand, the book contains much powerful, poetic prose and astute observations that ring real. Millett's account of the courtroom testimony is riveting. Some of *The Basement's* fictionalized passages are both lyrically intense and utterly believable: they "burn a hole in the page" (Nadine Gordimer once said this is the point of fiction) and mind.

Many readers of *The Basement*, both those who liked it and those annoyed by the author's fictionalizing, close the book yearning for a "just the facts" account of the case. That account is found in *The Indiana Torture Slaying*, a quickie paperback by reporter John Dean who was briefly called to testify at the trial. Millett got much of her information from this book and she properly gave him credit.

1966, the year when this book was published, was not a good time for books about true murder cases. It was put out by Bee-Line Books, a publisher specializing in cheap pornography with titles like Peekin Place, so it never found its proper audience.

Recently reissued by Borf Books, it is good journalism, written in a restrained and compassionate manner. There are problems with it, however. A student of the case whom this writer will call "Craig Kelley" complains that the "author almost canonizes Stephanie," a girl who, on at least one occasion, helped tie Sylvia up and who might have done more to check the outrages of her boyfriend, Coy Hubbard.

Mr. Kelley makes another good point when he says, "Dean just skips over a lot of really significant things. He reports that GB had only three spoons in the house and then goes on to something else."

The Likens case inspired a horror novel called *The Girl Next Door* by Jack Ketchum. Ketchum has turned the calendar back a bit, setting his tale in the 1950s. Pretty Meg and her sister Susan have been orphaned and sent to live with their Aunt Ruth Chandler, a mother of three boys whose home is a magnet for neighborhood kids. *The Girl Next Door* is a repulsively readable story. Ketchum has given the tale a haunting spin by having it narrated by David, a teenaged boy who watches Meg's tortures with a combined sense of titillation and disgust. Ketchum believably depicts David's confusion of conscience and his reluctance to take a stand against the others and stop the show—until it is too late.

Patte Wheat brought the story into the 1970s in By Sanction of the Victim. The story is told from the viewpoint of the victim, young Marjorie who is, along with her little brother Bruce and their dog Rocket, boarded at the home of Florrie Genoud. It is a powerful work of compassion and depth. Cofounders of Parents Anonymous, a group for potential or actual child abusers, give both a foreword and an afterword to the novel. However, the title, suggesting that the tormented child "sanctioned" her own abuse (a suggestion that is not made in the body of the work) is obscene.

It is possible, although not certain, that the Likens case served as an inspiration for Mendal Johnson's only novel, *Let's Go Play at the Adams.'* The parallels are not nearly as strong as in The Girl Next Door and By Sanction of the Victim. Johnson sets his story in affluent suburbia. There is no adult ringleader. A group of kids ranging in age from seventeen to ten tie up Barbara, their 20-year-old babys-itter. None of the moral accusations that were leveled against Sylvia—that she was a glutton, a thief, a slanderer, and a prostitute-figure in this novel. However, there is enough resemblance between the Adams' tale and the Likens murder to suggest a connection. The teenaged Dianne is described as "bony" like Mrs. Wright. The main torturers of Sylvia were two females and three males as is the case in Adams.' Finally, the murderers burn Barbara with a hot poker before finishing her off. They do not, however, make words out of the marks.

If Johnson was influenced by the Likens case, he, like Craig Kelly, saw it as "the ultimate example of how cruel children can be," a sort of *Lord of the Flies* scenario come to life. Mr. Kelly believes that the Likens torture "was about fun (twisted and perverted as it was). The neighborhood kids were having a great time. I think GB was a complete whacko and the kids were the major villains." After all, Mr. Kelly notes, Mrs. Wright lived in a house with ten people in it and only one spoon which convinced him that she was "a total basket case, incapable of raising children or managing life."

Although not about the Sylvia Likens case, a book called *Dear Corinne, Tell Somebody! Love, Annie* was inspired by it. It's author, poet, playwright, and composer Mari Evans, told *The Indianapolis Star* that she first became concerned about child abuse because of Likens' horrible death. Evans was deeply involved with the Black Arts Movement of the 1960s and her book is directed primarily at African American youngsters.

A never-published play called *Hey, Rube* was also inspired

by this slaying and that leads us to a most bizarre coincidence. The author of that play, Janet McReynolds, is the wife of the man who played Santa Claus at the Ramsey family's Christmas party just a couple of nights before six-year-old JonBenet Ramsey was murdered. Two of the factors in young JonBenet's life that may have played a role in her death were her bedwetting and the early sexualization of the tiny beauty queen, making the parallels to the murder of Sylvia Likens eerie indeed.

Bibliography

Archives of *The Indianapolis Star* and the defunct *The Indianapolis News*.

Dean, John. *The Indiana Torture Slaying: Sylvia Liken's Ordeal and Death*, Borf Books, Brownsville, KY, 1999.

Johnson, Mendal, *Let's Go Play at the Adams.'*

Ketchum, Jack. *The Girl Next Door, Overlook Connection Press*. Woodstock, GA. 1996.

Millett, Kate. *The Basement*. Simon and Schuster. New York. 1979.

Wheat, Patti. *By Sanction of the Victim.*

CHAPTER 2

The Honeymoon Killers Raymond Fernandez and "Obese Ogress" Martha Beck

Raymond Fernandez was born in Hawaii of Spanish immigrant parents in 1914. When Ray was three, his family moved to Connecticut. There his father ran into job discrimination because of his broken English and dark complexion. He worked intermittently at a series of low paid jobs. He saw another disappointment in his son who was often sickly and always frail.

Young Ray lacked the "macho" his father wanted in a male child. Frustrated, financially struggling, and disappointed, the "head of the household" drank heavily. He was a mean drunk who used excessive corporal punishment on Ray. The punishments escalated into beatings. Like many mistreated children, Ray developed a deep ambivalence toward his abuser. He feared his father's wrath yet admired the way he ruled as the undisputed king of his outwardly humble castle. If only Ray could be strong enough, masculine enough to make his father proud! But alas, the boy was stuck in a small-framed, non-muscular body.

The boy was self-conscious about many things, including his looks and his family's material deprivation. As an adolescent, he tried to assuage the sense of gnawing emptiness by stealing. Jailed at 15, the teenager decided to reverse the general movement of immigration: he would leave America for Spain, the land of his forebears, and make a fresh start there.

Upon his release, he did exactly that. Relatives in the old

country were willing to take Ray in, and he settled down and grew to adulthood in Spain.

The Great Depression hit the United States and Ray's father believed he had had enough of life in the supposed land of opportunity. He wanted to re-establish a relationship with his son so he wrote to Ray and told him of his desires. His mother and father joined him in Spain. They found that their son had become a well-liked young man. He had a calm, genial manner that easily won him friends, especially among women. The thin lanky physique that his father had often frowned upon brought a smile to many a feminine mouth.

When Fernandez was about 20 years old, he married Encarnación Robles and fathered a child with her. The financially troubled couple argued frequently and Fernandez solved his marital problems as he previously had solved his legal ones, by leaving the country. Almost as soon as he got back to America, Encarnación wrote to him that their young son was very sick.

Alarmed, Fernandez took the first boat back to Spain. There he found a country ripped apart by Civil War. He enlisted in Franco's army. After Franco's victory, Fernandez drifted from job to job. He was never a good breadwinner for his wife and son but did the best he could. He was a gardener and a garbage collector and did other tasks both manual and menial.

When World War II started, Fernandez saw an opportunity. In 1939, he traveled to Gibraltar and set up as an ice-cream vendor, selling this goodie to British military personnel and tourists.

One day a British man asked to speak privately with the ice-cream seller. Perhaps he recognized that the extroverted man who easily made friends could be of special use. He explained that he was from British Intelligence and said, "We can use you provided you are capable of obeying orders and being discreet." Fernandez assured the questioner he was and he became a low-level spy for the Allies. Precisely what he did remains obscure but Fernandez appears to have demonstrated intelligence and courage to his spymasters. In an article published in Killer Couples, Bruce Sander, quotes glowing testimonial that British Intelligence presented to the spy, "Raymond Fernandez was entirely loyal to the Allied cause and carried out his duties, which were sometimes difficult and dangerous, extremely well."

After the war, the ex-spy did not want to return to his life as a humdrum laborer and family man. He signed on with a ship, for a life of high-spirited adventure. Instead, he had an accident that would drastically alter his life. A hatch cover slammed across his head, cracking his skull. The accident sheared off much of the thick, black hair he had been so proud and left gruesome scars in its place. After this misfortune, Fernandez suffered severe headaches and a personality change. Acquaintances believed his general demeanor and conduct worsened. Where he had previously been calm and controlled, he became grumpy and sullen, flying into a rage at the slightest provocation. Perhaps the worst damage done was to his ego. Insecure as a child, he found comfort in knowing that women found him attractive and he knew that his abundant dark hair was part of his appeal. Being partially bald and scarred must have reawakened the insecurities of his childhood.

The ship he boarded sailed for the United States of America but Fernandez first re-visited the nation of his childhood from a jail cell because he had stolen some items from the vessel. After a year behind bars, Fernandez went to Brooklyn to look up his sister. The kind-hearted woman gave her brother shelter and he gave her a hard time. Unable to find employment, he was generally in a bad temper and often verbally lashed out at her.

During this period, Fernandez practiced voodoo. His sister was disconcerted by the odor of incense that frequently wafted from his room as well as the indecipherable chanting he uttered as he knelt before his makeshift voodoo altar. According to Sander, Fernandez told his sister "a fantastic story about learning Voodoo spells and rites from a prisoner in Tallahassee with whom he had become friendly." He also claimed he learned to "hypnotize folks from a distance" and "make women do what I want by thought concentration."

Fernandez's sister scoffed at his bragging. But Fernandez was to show that he did have a certain baffling power over some members of the female gender.

He wrote to several members of various lonely-hearts clubs. In 1947, he began writing to Jane Thompson. Thompson's marriage had recently collapsed. Bespectacled and plain-faced, she was not sure she would be able to find another husband and a life of solitude frightened her. The letters from Fernandez impressed her with their tone of gentle caring. She was excited by his romantic approach: he asked for a lock of her hair! She was delighted to send it to him. She did not know that the hair was for a voodoo spell that Fernandez believed would put a woman completely under his power. Soon they arranged a meeting.

Wearing a toupee of thick, black hair, Fernandez was gratified to find Thompson falling under his "spell." While Fernandez attributed his success with women to voodoo, it is more likely his firm belief in it helped him radiate the confidence many women found appealing. Fernandez had a gut-level understanding of female needs and knew how to make a woman feel that he desired her. He gazed at each woman as if he were utterly enthralled by her and his piercing dark eyes seemed to turn into mirrors that reflected an image of youth and beauty to women who were often insecure, aging, and homely. He knew not to give the impression he was out after sex but appeared to care about her as a person.

The couple traveled to Spain on her nickel pretending to be married. Strangely, Fernandez took Thompson to meet his real wife—after he convinced Mrs. Fernandez to allow herself to be introduced as an old friend named "Señora Robles." Why would Encarnación participate in such a bizarre deception, especially when it was so demeaning to her? Fernandez had a knack for convincing women he was madly in love with them and appeared sincere even when spouting outrageous lies. It is a common practice among con artists to play on the larcenous spirit in their victims.

Perhaps he told his wife he needed to get money from Thompson so he could support his wife and their young son.

If he pulled this off, he would settle down with the woman he deeply loved and had pined for, Encarnación. The odd trio went out to restaurants, theaters, and bullfights without Thompson ever suspecting his old friend was really his wife and the mother of his child. However, one day Fernandez and Thompson had a loud, raucous argument in a hotel room. Thompson was found dead the next morning of digitalis poisoning. Police suspected her "husband" but could not question him because Fernandez took the first boat back to America before his lover's corpse was cold.

In the U.S., he scammed Jane Thompson's mother. After several hours, he was able to draw a good facsimile of Thompson's signature affixed to a document purporting to be her last will and testament, leaving everything to Ray Fernandez. He sought out her mother, Mrs. Wilson, and waved the document in her face. His appearance of sincerity and conviction gulled her into believing it genuine.

The document scared Mrs. Wilson. It said that the home she shared with her daughter belonged to him. He assured her he was not going to make her leave—after all, she was the mother of a woman who had been very dear to him. The two of them could share the home. "I shall see that you are not disturbed," he said. "Things for you will continue just as before." The older woman was grateful to the man who seemed so caring and considerate. Her daughter must have been lucky to be loved by such a kind, generous person.

While living there, Fernandez continued writing to lonely-hearts club members stealing dollars, checks, jewelry, and whatever of value he could grab. His victims were not wealthy so his takes were never high but he was able to make a living through the sheer number of swindles. The women he conned were single when unmarried women were still being called "spinsters" with no sense of irony.

They yearned for passion, which Fernandez seemed to bring, and marriage that he routinely promised. When they realized that they had been taken, they were too ashamed to go to the police. They would have had to reveal themselves as fools and, perhaps even worse, to tell the police they shared physical intimacies with a man to whom they were not married.

On one of these swindling sorties, he encountered a woman who was to change his life, a very lonely, sensuous, dark-haired, 300-pound nurse named Martha Beck.

Sad Martha

Born Martha Seabrook in Milton, Florida on May 6, 1920, she came into the world with a glandular problem that caused her to be morbidly obese, and she was endlessly teased and jeered by her schoolmates. Her father deserted the family while she was a toddler. To compound her problems, her brother sexually assaulted her when she was 13 years old.

Martha was accepted by a school of nursing. She graduated first in her class in 1942. Martha Seabrook was going to succeed. However, she had difficulty getting employment despite her qualifications. She attributed this to her weight. Finally, an undertaker hired her to prepare corpses. The job was a bitter disappointment. Seabrook had honed her skills in nursing school and knew that she could give good care to patients. Yet, she could only get a job working with those no longer able to benefit from her care.

The lonely woman escaped the disappointment and failure of her life by reading true romance magazines. She also frequented theaters to watch movies like The Garden of Allah and Gaslight that starred her favorite actor, Charles Boyer.

After eight months of working for the mortician, Seabrook heard there was a nurse shortage in California and decided to take her chances. Shortly after her arrival in the sunshine state, she got a job at a hospital.

Seabrook started to partially live out the fantasies of romance she had nurtured for so long. She had an affair with a bus driver. Soon the 20-something nurse found herself pregnant and demanded her boyfriend marry her. He put her off, and then attempted suicide by throwing himself into the Pacific Ocean. Rescuers pulled him out but he made a hurried and complete exit from Seabrook's life. Seabrook was unable to track him down when her mind snapped under the stress of an unwed pregnancy in an era when it was a disgrace. She was hospitalized for psychiatric reasons.

She appeared to recover after a few days. Then she behaved sensibly, moving to Pensacola, Florida, so she could put on a ring and pretend to be the wife of a soldier away in the war. Around the time of her baby's birth, she sent herself a phony telegram saying her husband had been killed in action.

The new mother and ersatz war widow found herself a genuine beau by the name of Alfred Beck. Oddly, like the father of her child, he was a bus driver. The two soon married but Beck divorced Martha within a year, when she was pregnant with her second child.

Although her personal life was again bleak, Martha's career took a turn for the better. The Pensacola Crippled Children's Home hired her. She did so well she was promoted to superintendent. She was making something of herself as a nurse.

Perhaps her on-the-job success encouraged Beck to take another chance on love. She joined Mother Dinene's Family Club for Lonely Hearts and received a letter from Ray Fernandez. She took a liking to the man whose epistles were so courtly and charming.

Unbridled Passion

After corresponding regularly for a while, they agreed to meet in Florida. When Beck saw the thin, black-haired gentleman who had written her such flowery letters, she fell head over heels. She thought he resembled her idol, Charles Boyer. Surprisingly, Fernandez, accustomed to deceiving women only to bilk them out of bucks, was smitten as well. Most articles about the case say that Fernandez was attracted to Beck "despite" her weight. However, it seems equally possible that he was attracted to her because of it. At any rate, the couple spent many steamy hours in hotel rooms gratifying their mutual passion.

Fernandez soon realized Beck had no money and no property. After two days of sensual bliss, he wanted to return to women who would gratify his greed instead of his lust. He made an excuse to Beck and headed back to New York. From the Big Apple, he wrote his lover a "Dear Johnette" letter. The epistle devastated Beck but it was only the beginning of her troubles.

Word about Beck's hotel trysts got back to the board of the Pensacola Crippled Children's Home. The era was one in which "moral turpitude" was grounds for firing and Beck got the axe. Unemployed and bereft of her love, saddled with the care and support of two little children, the frightened and angry woman determined that wily little Ray Fernandez would be her salvation whether he liked it or not.

The unemployed single mother packed her bags, took her kids, and headed for Fernandez's home. Fernandez's reaction to these uninvited and unannounced visitors was to take them in. What could those reasons have been? Fernandez was used to loving and leaving women—after fleecing them. They were suckers but not this woman. She wanted to impose on him. That was a switch. The demanding, take-no-nonsense Beck had a will as strong as his. Her portly size may have inflamed his erotic passion while her brashness aroused deeper emotions, perhaps even a kind of respect.

Fernandez soon concluded the apartment they shared with Jane Thompson's mother was too crowded. He told her, if she were going to stay with him, the kids would have to go. Beck did not want to be an out of work single mother. Even more, she did not want to lose Fernandez for with him she was living the love she had read about in romance magazines. He was her Charles Boyer, just as handsome and charming and a thousand times more precious because he could hold her in his arms. The kids were packed off to Beck's relatives in Florida. Not long thereafter, Mrs. Wilson also vacated. Beck may have given her the creeps and, if so, Wilson can be credited with astute judgement.

To Fernandez's surprise, Beck was not upset when he told

her he had been a swindling woman through lonely-hearts clubs. Instead, she wanted to join him in the fleecing. Sanders' analysis was probably right on target when he wrote that "She had suddenly seen an opportunity for hitting back at her own sex, for squaring the long overdue account for all the humiliation and misery she had suffered from the years of tender girlhood."

The pigeons represented every skinny girl who had taunted her, every slender woman who had a husband while she had only True Romance, and all the women hired over her who were favored because they were at an acceptable weight. She would be deceiving women into thinking they had this wonderful, entrancing man while she would know he was really hers. Beck would pose as Fernandez's sister when they met victims.

Their first mutual mark was a Pennsylvania schoolteacher named Esther Henne. This "unclaimed blessing" exchanged several letters with Fernandez and was impressed by the eloquence, interest, and concern his epistles radiated. The woman was convinced that she had found true love and connubial bliss would follow. The skinny suitor visited his amour with his full-figured sister in tow.

Fernandez proposed marriage and the teacher accepted. She found herself on a strange honeymoon, however. Each night, her groom retired to his own bedroom while the bride shared sleeping quarters with her supposed sister-in-law. When the wife objected to this bizarre arrangement, Beck became intimidating which was not hard given that there was a considerable size difference between the two women. The three returned to New York. The wife discovered that her finances had been bled dry but was too frightened to confront Fernandez and Beck. Instead, she just left.

Sanders wrote, "For two years these confidence tricksters worked at their cruel and unrelenting racket, duping the gullible into mock marriages with the alleged brother, and then extracting their personal wealth and making life so generally intolerable that the dupes were glad to decamp."

In 1948, they found a pigeon too feisty to do as she was

told and then get out of the way. Middle-aged widow Myrtle Young of Greene Forrest, Arkansas, hoped life was not passing her by when she started exchanging letters with the dashing, romantic Fernandez, she had a new lease on life. His marriage proposal was eagerly accepted. In August, she traveled to Cook County, Illinois, where she and her thick-haired Latin Romeo wed.

Young was outraged when her ostensible sister-in-law insisted on sharing her honeymoon bed. Beck forced the woman to take a heavy dosage of barbiturates. Then she and Fernandez put the semi-conscious woman on a bus headed for Little Rock, Arkansas. When the bus pulled into the depot, those around her realized Young was not in an ordinary sleep and rushed her to the hospital where she died shortly after her arrival. She was unable to share with police the story of her strange honeymoon and coerced doping.

Did Beck and Fernandez intend to kill Young? That cannot be answered although they were willing to risk it when they forced barbiturates on her. They would commit quite deliberate murders soon after this crime.

Although nothing was proven about the death of Jane Thompson, it is possible Fernandez murdered before he met Beck. There are no reports of Beck's being violent before her association with Fernandez. By herself, she was pitiful; with him, she was murderous. Beck falls into the pattern of a previously non-criminal woman whose sociopathic tendencies are unleashed through her relationship with a dominant, homicidal man. Bonnie Parker may be the prime example of this sort of female criminality. Caril Fugate, who followed boyfriend Charlie Starkweather into spree killing and Myra Hindley, who became a child killer at lover Ian Brady's behest, are other examples.

In no case should it be assumed the women were previously "normal" or that going along with murder was simply a matter of the submission to the man's wishes. Women with strong moral codes would give a firm "no" to a murderous partner. Rather, these women had destructive desires that might have remained untapped had they not met the men that they did.

Why did Beck and Fernandez prey on women? Beck had a grudge against other women. Females often feel they in competition for males and Beck had been unfairly passed over for slimmer women in work and love. Fernandez, abused as a child by a man, had feelings toward his domineering father that included admiration, envy, a desire to impress, fear and loathing. It is probable he was contemptuous of his weak, ineffectual mother who watched her son being bullied and beaten but did nothing to protect him. His mother put up with alcoholism and child abuse rather than risk losing her husband.

His victims wanted marriage so badly they believed his lies. "Fools deserve whatever they get," is the con artist's classic creed. Fernandez expanded it to cover those whose lives he took.

Fernandez and Beck continued pulling cons.

Using the alias "Charles Martin," he began writing to a 66-year-old widow in Albany named Janet Fay. Fay knew that she was long past the age when women are usually regarded as being attractive but she still hoped for someone with whom to share her life. She lived in a large apartment; it was too big for one person and reinforced her sense of loneliness. A deeply religious Roman Catholic who faithfully attended mass, Fay was pleased to find that this eloquent and refined Charles Martin shared her beliefs. His letters were filled with references to God, Jesus Christ, and the church. She was thrilled when he asked for a lock of her hair. They arranged to meet in December 1948. Fernandez altered his appearance to make himself look older. He put white streaks in his hair and make-up to deepen lines around his eyes. In late December, Martin and his "sister" traveled to Albany to meet Fay. The courtly gentleman showed up on Fay's doorstep carrying a bouquet of flowers. They spent much of their time sharing their similar religious convictions.

As the New Year of 1949 rolled around, Fay found herself entranced by this smooth-talking, and deeply Christian man. So smitten she agreed to give all her cash, bonds, and jewelry to the man she thought of as her husband-to-be. Martin's helpful sister packed it in the trunk had been the property of the late Myrtle Young.

Fay probably anticipated a romantic elopement when she set off with her fiancé and future sister-in-law for the small town of Valley Stream. The trio rented a little apartment. Settling into her new digs, Fay spoke of writing to her stepdaughter. Beck reacted sourly to the idea and harsh words were exchanged.

Suddenly the 300-pound nurse grabbed a hammer and slammed Fay's head with it. The elderly woman's skull cracked but she did not die instantly. As blood flowed from her head, Fernandez strangled her. False teeth plopped out of her mouth as she died. Nonplussed, Beck shoved the corpse into a cupboard and got rid of the dentures. Beck and Fernandez sat around discussing ways to get rid of the body. Fernandez mentioned his sister in Astoria lived in a home with a big basement. Myrtle Young's trunk was not big enough to hold Janet Fay so they bought a new one, and then headed for his sister's house.

Could they leave the trunk in her cellar for a little while they asked? Certainly, his sister replied. The January weather was freezing so Beck figured the body would keep for a few days before giving off a telltale odor. Fernandez and Beck rented a house in Queens that had a cellar then fetched the trunk from his sister's home. They buried Fay in a hole in the basement they filled over with cement. When the cement hardened after a few days, the couple went to the real estate agent to say they did not want the house after all.

Beck wanted Fay's property from American Express but knew it might set off alarms if they did it themselves. She believed she could persuade Janet's stepdaughter to help them. Thus, she typed the following letter and mailed it to that stepdaughter, Mary Spencer.

Dear Mary, I am all excited and having the time of my life. I never felt so happy before. I soon will be Mrs. Martin, and go to Florida. Mary, I am about to ask you a great favor. I would like you to call on the American Express Agency and have them ship my trunks and boxes that I have there to me. The address is on the various stickers I am enclosing in the letter. I would like to sort out many things before I leave for Florida. I am so happy and contented, for Charles is so good and nice to me and also his family. They have done everything to make me feel comfortable and at home. I will close with my best wishes for you both and love and kisses for the children. I really do miss you all, but I am sure that my prayers are granted to me by sending me this wonderful man. God bless you all. Janet J. Fay

Spencer immediately spotted this letter for a phony. She knew her stepmother could not type and the formal signature jarred. She went to the police with her suspicions.

In the meantime, Fernandez and Beck traveled to Grand Rapids, Michigan so he could meet 41-year-old Delphine Downing, a widow he was courting through a lonely-hearts club. Downing had lost her husband in the recent war. She wanted to remarry but feared that eligible men would not be interested in a ready-made family and would run when they learned of Rainelle. She was pleased Fernandez had not lost interest when she told him she was the mother of a toddler. Delphine introduced the pair to her almost two-year-old daughter Rainelle and allowed "brother and sister" to stay in her home so she and Fernandez could become better acquainted. Fernandez entranced by little Rainelle spent time playing with her. The debonair Latin who courted her in such a thoughtful, romantic manner equally entranced the child's mother.

One evening at Delphine's home, Fernandez was relaxing and reading the newspaper. He had kicked off his shoes and removed his toupee. Suddenly the door opened. A stunned Delphine Downing exclaimed, "You're bald!" Upset by the look of disappointment on her face, Fernandez said, "Look, honey, you don't have to act this way because I cover a bald patch. Heck, it's no crime, Delphie."

She had thought he was suave, handsome, and young. She shrank from his approach. "Don't touch me, you imposter!" she cried. "Why, you're old. Old!" He tried to sweet talk her but she ordered both he and his "sister" to leave immediately.

Fernandez grabbed but she struggled out of his grasp and ran into 300-pound Beck, attracted by the commotion. Accounts differ as to what transpired next. One of those versions holds that Fernandez took a pistol out of his jacket pocket, and shot Delphine Dowling in the head. She slid to the floor as Fernandez watched her last breath, his mind was not on her death, but on the disgust she had recently hurled his way. "Martha," he said plaintively, "she saw me without the toupee and said I was old. She didn't want me. She said we had to leave tonight. Martha, you don't think I'm old—not too old?" She took him in her arms, held his long lean head against her well-endowed chest, and gave him the reassurance he craved. Of course, he was still attractive, still youthful, she told him.

A baby's cry disturbed this loving scene.

Beck told Fernandez they should take care of this the way they had Janet Fay. He should dig a hole in the cellar big enough for mother and child. The former nurse and mother of two filled a bathtub with water to drown little Rainelle Dowling. After breaking through the thin layer of cement in the basement with his shovel, Fernandez dug out a little pit. Delphine was shoved inside it along with her dead baby and it was covered over. Another version of the Downing murders maintains they were stretched out over a couple of days. When Delphine ran into Beck, the "sister" tried to soothe her and convinced her to take sleeping pills.

Rainelle saw her mother in an unnatural sleep and started crying. A frazzled Beck choked the girl into unconsciousness but not death. Fernandez believed they had to kill Delphine.

"If she wakes up and sees Rainelle," he pointed out, "she'll go to the police." Then he grabbed the gun that belonged to Delphine's late husband, put it against her head, and pulled the trigger. Rainelle regained consciousness and saw her mother being slaughtered. Fernandez and Beck carried the mother's body into the basement and buried it. For two days, they took care of little Rainelle as the confused and terrified little girl cried and could not eat. Finally, Fernandez decided that their only course was to kill the baby, too.

He ordered Beck to murder Rainelle.

"I can't do it, Ray!" Beck said. "I can't."

Fernandez told her she would. Reluctantly, she complied, drowning the child, then helping Fernandez bury her beside her mother in the cellar. Although accounts differ about the Downing killings, there is not dispute about what Fernandez and Beck did after killing Rainelle. The deadly duo capped the night off with a trip to a theater to take in a movie where they enjoyed sodas and popcorn along with the show.

They returned home tired and eager to sleep. Fernandez and Beck did not have time to settle into bed before they heard a knock on the door. Fernandez answered. Police officers on the porch invited themselves in. What were they there for? Fernandez wondered. They could not possibly know what had happened to Delphine and Rainelle Dowling—could they? "You Raymond Fernandez?" a policeman asked. "You ever know a Mrs. Janet Fay?" Fernandez was too scared to answer. Beck saw the police and said, "Leave him alone. Don't you goddamn cops touch Ray or I'll—" She made threats but was not able to act on them before being clapped into handcuffs. Police found the bodies of mother and infant buried in the cellar.

The story of the Lonely Hearts Killers made headlines across the nation. While only these three murders would be officially established as theirs, there were persistent rumors that they had done away with other pigeons. Some estimates say they killed as many as twelve people.

Both murderers seemed less concerned with the possible death sentence than their reputations. Fernandez told investigators, "I'm no average killer! I have a way with women, a power over them."

Beck was distraught by terms like "Obese Ogress" with which she was tagged by the newspapers. "I'm still a human being," she protested, "feeling every blow inside, even though I have the ability to hide my feelings and laugh. But that doesn't say my heart isn't breaking from the insults and humiliation of being talked about as I am."

When they were in custody, a dispute arose between Michigan and New York as to which state would try them.

Michigan had no death penalty while New York had a busy electric chair. Roger McMahon, district attorney of Michigan's Kent County, used their fear of New York's death penalty to persuade them to sing a 73-page confession. He promised that they would not be extradited to New York if they did. McMahon lied. Michigan allowed them to be extradited to New York so they would face the ultimate penalty for the murder of Janet Fay.

They went on trial in the middle of 1949's simmering heat wave. The weather did not keep intrigued spectators from crowding into the courtroom where they sat, cheek by jowl, wiping sweat off their foreheads and fanning themselves while listening to testimony about sex and deception, mayhem and murder. Judge Ferdinand Pecora heard the case. He was reputed to be a no-nonsense jurist who did not allow a case to be bogged down in irrelevant details. Nassau County District Attorney Edward Robinson, Jr. (not the famous actor) prosecuted them. He put a variety of witnesses on the stand, including the medical examiner who autopsied Janet Fay, detectives and forensic experts, relatives, and friends of the victim.

Herbert Rosenberg defended both Beck and Fernandez. He called Fernandez to the stand July 11, 1949. He said he had had nothing to do with Fay's death. He admitted confessing to it when questioned by the police in Michigan but claimed he was only being chivalrous, taking the blame so his ladylove could go free. "All my statements were made for the purpose of helping Martha," he testified. Apparently, the prospect of electrocution had led him to discard his wish to shield the woman he loved.

Robinson tore into the defendant on cross-examination. He questioned him about Jane Thompson, Myrtle Young, Delphine Downing, and her daughter Rainelle. He grew louder and louder in his outrage until Ray's co-defendant shouted, "Mr. Fernandez is not deaf!"

The witness admitted he had shot and killed Delphine Downing but denied murdering Janet Fay. That led to another outburst from an agitated Beck. "I think at this time," she told Judge Pecora as she rose to her feet, "I want to take the stand!

The judge admonished her not to talk out of turn. Rosenberg called her as a witness early in the morning of July 25, 1945. Wearing a gray and white polka dot dress and a double-strand pearl necklace, the "Obese Ogress" took the stand. Her lawyer took her through her background as a teased youngster and her adulthood of disappointments.

He led her to her relationship with Fernandez and her agreement to become his criminal confederate. Finally, her testimony turned to the murder of Janet Fay. Beck remembered Fernandez telling her to keep the woman quiet. Then she was amnesiac.

The next thing she recalled, she was standing over a dead Fay and Fernandez was shaking her shoulders, asking, "My God, Martha, what have you done?" If Beck had killed Janet Fay, it was due to her deep love for Fernandez. When the prosecutor questioned her, she said, "We loved each other and I consider it absolutely sacred." Later she stated, "a request from Mr. Fernandez to me is a command. I loved him enough to do anything he asked me to."

The Lonely-Hearts case went to the jury on August 18, 1949. They began deliberating at 9:45 p.m. and had a verdict by 8:30 a.m. the next morning. Both defendants were convicted of first-degree murder. The jury did not recommend mercy. On August 22, Judge Pecora sentenced Raymond Fernandez and Martha Beck to death in the electric chair. It would be almost two years before the sentence was carried out.

While awaiting execution, Martha wrote poetry. An example follows.

Memo to Ray

Remember, sweetheart, the night that you and I Side by side were sitting. Watching o'er the moonlit sky Fleecy clouds were flitting, How close our hands were linked then, When, my darling, when will they be linked again? What to me the starlight still Or the moonbeam's splendour, If I do not feel the thrill of your fingers tender?

The poem was shown to Ray who was moved to tears. He took pencil to paper and scrawled a note for her. "I would like to shout my love for you to the world."

The bizarre couple was executed at Sing Sing on March 8, 1951.

On the last day of her life, Martha Beck set a goal for herself and, pitifully, failed to keep it. She was tired of hearing people ridicule her as a glutton so she would deliberately show them possessed self-control by not overdoing her last meal. Then she changed her mind and asked for a double order of everything, wolfing down heaping helpings of salads, fried potatoes, and chicken. Unlike Fernandez, she showed a certain amount of courage since she walked to the electric chair on her own. Fernandez collapsed on the death day. In keeping with the tradition of executing the more distraught prisoner first, guards carried him into the death chamber before Martha.

The Martha Beck/Raymond Fernandez affair was the basis of a film called *The Honeymoon Killers*, made in the 1970s. Starring Shirley Stoler and Tony Lo Bianco and written and directed by Leonard Kastle, it stuck pretty close to the facts and became a cult classic for its daring (by contemporary standards) depictions of sex and violence. The couple was again cinematically portrayed in 1996 when acclaimed Mexican director Arturo Ripstein came out with *Deep Crimson*.

There have been other homicidal couples but none as unlikely as Raymond Fernandez and Martha Beck. Their union was distinguished by their viciousness toward other people and, paradoxically, their devotion to each other. Fiction can imitate and dramatize but not outdo the singular passion and perversity of the Lonely-Hearts Killers.

Bibliography

Buck, Paul. *The Honeymoon Killers*. Universal-Award House, Inc. New York, NY. 1970.

Crimelibrary.com. *Serial Killers.*

Everitt, David. *Human Monsters.* Contemporary Books. Chicago, IL. 1993.

Jones, Richard Glyn. *Killer Couples.* Berkley Books, New York, NY 1987.

Newton, Michael. *Bad Girls Do It!* Loompanics Unlimited, Port Townsend, WA. 1993.

CHAPTER 3

Fumiko Kimura, a Mother Who Tried to Kill Herself and Did Kill Her Children

The sun was out but the temperature was chilly on Tuesday, January 29, 1985, as Loyola Marymount University students Nancy Pontius and Kevin Silva strolled along the seashore of the Santa Monica, California beach. Suddenly they noticed something thick and dark atop the water. At first they thought they might be looking at a mass of seaweed. The puzzled college students motioned to joggers Brian Hirsch and Arthur Brock to stop. All four stared at the configuration in the water. One of the joggers climbed on the other's shoulders to get a better look, and then exclaimed, "It looks like a body!"

An arm flew up, confirming this observation.

After a quick conference, it was agreed that the joggers would try to get other help while Nancy and Kevin attempted an immediate rescue.

The joggers ran to phone authorities.

Nancy and Kevin raced fully clothed into the water. Kevin grabbed a six-month-old baby and carried her to the shore. Nancy took hold of a four-year-old boy and carried him there as well. Then Kevin waded back into the water and pulled out the children's mother, Fumiko Kimura, 32. While Kevin was in the water, Nancy held a hand of each child. Of Yuri, she recalled, "I felt at that moment like that baby was my baby."

The eyes of all three partially drowned people were open and staring as Kevin and Nancy frantically began clearing foam out of their mouths and pushing on their bellies.

"Live! Live! Please, live!" Nancy screamed.

Rushed to the hospital, all three were alive on arrival. Kazutaka died later that day.

Medical personnel found that Yuri suffered brain damage when she arrived at the hospital. She was listed in critical condition and put on a life-support system.

She died four days later on February 2.

Only Fumiko recovered. There were reports that she was not grateful to her rescuers, bitterly saying, "They must have been Caucasians. Otherwise, they would have let me die."

Traumas of Divorce, Abortion, Divorce

This double infanticide and attempted suicide was the nadir of a life that to Fumiko seemed scarred by repeated failures.

Born and raised in Japan, Fumiko had been one of six children. Her childhood was normal in most respects. She enjoyed sports and music and especially liked playing the piano. She also made friends easily. However, her family has said that even as a child Fumiko was "prone to self-criticism."

As a child, she suffered a major trauma when her parents divorced. Her mother remarried but Fumiko did not bond with her stepfather. As an unmarried teenager, Fumiko suffered another major trauma when she became pregnant. In a culture that highly values female chastity, an out of wedlock birth threatens disgrace. Fumiko had to feel that she had failed her family by becoming pregnant without being married.

Fumiko had an abortion. This is hardly the place to discuss the politics of whether abortion should be legal or illegal. However, it is safe to say that while carrying to term may be psychologically devastating or even impossible for some females with problem pregnancies, having an abortion is not without physical and psychological cost. Those who abort are often tormented by deep feelings of guilt and grief and haunted by nagging might-have-beens.

In 1972, when she was 20, Fumiko traveled to Los Angeles, California to study music at Glendale Community College.

She hoped for an eventual career as a piano player. She married soon after her arrival in the U.S. The marriage ended in divorce after three years. She worked as a restaurant server in 1980 when she met sushi chef Itsuroku Kimura, also a Japanese immigrant.

Itsuroku had come to America the previous year. He had a passion for painting. Perhaps they were drawn to each in part because of their shared artistic leanings as well as the bond of being Japanese immigrants to America. They were soon dating regularly and decided to wed.

When Itsuroku and Fumiko married, she quit paid work for fulltime homemaking although she still enjoyed playing her piano. Since Itsuroku was not financially successful with his art, he concentrated on the restaurant business. Soon after their marriage, he became co-owner of a restaurant called Tokyo West.

Fumiko gave birth to son Kazutaka in 1980. Fearing he might hurt himself if he fell against something hard, Fumiko got rid of much furniture including the piano she loved to play.

The well-organized Fumiko wrote a schedule of each day's planned activities. In that schedule, she designated specific times for domestic chores such as cleaning and cooking as well as maternal activities such as playing with her son.

Daughter Yuri arrived in July 1984. Late in this pregnancy, Fumiko's mother, Yoshiko Higa, traveled to California to visit the family. She stayed until November 1985.

Yoshiko thought Fumiko became depressed after her second child's birth. "There was a darkness to her face," Yoshiko recalled. "Her hair was falling out. I thought it was just because of the birth and she would get better."

A *Los Angeles Times* article reported, "While nursing her daughter, Fumiko would get up in the middle of the night to eat soup, concerned that she was properly nourishing her baby."

Although she had made friends easily as a child, the adult Fumiko had few confidants.

Fumiko and Itsuroku kept up Japanese traditions. The

family slept on mats rather than beds. Shoes were left by the door. They usually spoke English in public but Japanese at home.

When Fumiko took her children to the pediatrician, both she and little Kazutaka would bow their heads in a traditional Japanese manner of showing respect.

Fumiko did not drive so she and the children made trips by public transit.

Whenever her husband came home, Fumiko washed his feet, again keeping up a Japanese tradition. Even if he came home from the restaurant very late, she would stay up so she could perform this task.

Although shy, Fumiko was no recluse. Neighbors often saw her outdoors with her children. She frequently sat on a bench at the apartment complex playground, holding baby Yuri, while Kazutaka merrily rode his tricycle around the pavement.

A Revelation Precipitates Crisis

One day in mid-January 1985, Fumiko received a phone call from a stranger. The caller was a female Japanese immigrant who confessed that she had been enjoying a romantic relationship with Itsuroku for the past three years. A classically "kept" mistress, she lived in an apartment Itsuroku paid for and in which he visited her about three times a week. The woman wanted to break off the relationship but believed Fumiko was entitled to know of her husband's infidelity. The mistress, Kazue Tanahashi, visited the Kimuras and the three of them discussed the situation. Fumiko learned that Itsuroku had impregnated Kazue who had aborted the pregnancy.

The story of Kazue's abortion may have ripped open the wounds left by Fumiko's own abortion.

In the days after this discussion, Fumiko had trouble sleeping and began drinking the Japanese wine sake to combat her insomnia and her anxiety. Then she saw a doctor to obtain sleeping medicine. She could no longer breastfeed and fretted that Yuri was losing weight now that she had to rely on formula.

On January 27, Fumiko telephoned family members in Japan who were alarmed by how irrational she sounded, bouncing from one subject to another and making little sense.

The next day, a messenger arrived at the Kimura home with a note for Fumiko. It was from her husband's girlfriend who apologized for the affair and offered to commit suicide if it would help heal the family's wounds.

Fumiko made no reply to this message.

On January 28, a neighbor visited Fumiko. Although Fumiko wore a watch, she repeatedly asked her visitor for the time. She appeared distraught and distracted. To aggravate matters even more, Kazutaka was sick with a cold.

That evening Itsuroku did not come home until 2:00 a.m. As usual, his wife had waited up so she could wash his feet.

The next day—ten days after learning of her husband's affair—Fumiko told Itsuroku that she was taking Yuri to the pediatrician for a check-up and would take the sickly Kazutaka as well.

Before Itsuroku left for work, Fumiko kissed her unfaithful husband and said, "Please go and come safely."

Since the weather was chilly, she dressed the youngsters in warm clothes. Fumiko did not drive so she and her children boarded a bus. However, it was not bound for a doctor's office but the Santa Monica beach. The trio transferred twice between buses and it took them two hours to reach Fumiko's destination. Since it was early morning, the beach was almost deserted. Fumiko carried Yuri and held Kazutaka's hand, leading them past a Cocky Moon hotdog stand and a shooting gallery.

Even though he had a cold, the energetic Kazutaka ran and played with the sand. His mother took his hand firmly again.

She led him and carried his baby sister into the water and waded until she was deep inside it. Then she put her head under the water, opened her mouth and repeatedly gulped salty water. As she was doing this, she held her children's heads underwater. Bruises found on their bodies showed that the terrified children fought desperately for their lives as their mother drowned them.

Then the college students mentioned at the start of this article saw what they first thought was a mass of seaweed.

When Itsuroku came home that evening, he was surprised to find his wife and children gone from home. While searching for them, he discovered his daughter's stroller abandoned near a bus stop.

Did She Kill Kids Rather than Become a Witch?

Japan has traditionally viewed suicide as an honorable way out of disgrace. While viewed as cowardly in the West, it is seen as courageous in that nation. However, the mother of small children who commits suicide and leaves her children orphaned is seen negatively.

She is considered a witch or demon whose soul will never have peace. It is possible that this belief evolved to prevent Japanese mothers from resorting to suicide. Sadly, its practical effect is that suicidal mothers are likely to kill their children in what is called oyako-shinju or parent-child suicide. Although such actions are illegal in Japan, a parent who killed his or her children during a suicide attempt would usually be leniently treated by the Japanese legal system.

Even while Fumiko languished in the hospital, there was an outpouring of sympathy for her. Los Angeles County assistant district attorney Louise Comar noted, "People feel badly for Mrs. Kimura." Despite that sympathy, Fumiko was charged with two counts of first-degree murder "with special circumstances"—those circumstances in this case being multiple victims—which made her eligible for either life imprisonment with no possibility of parole or the death penalty.

Japanese immigrants and Japanese-Americans joined to form the Fumiko Kimura Fair Trial Committee. A *Chicago Tribune* article noted, "Her supporters are asking that the American legal system take Kimura's cultural heritage into consideration when the case is tried. So far they have collected more than 1,000 signatures on petitions asking the district attorney to charge Kimura with involuntary manslaughter instead of first-degree murder, and to grant her a probated sentence with 'supervised rehabilitation.'"

Japanese-American attorney Mike Yamaki commented on the seeming absurdity of sentencing someone to death who had attempted suicide. "The State of California is going to spend money to put this woman to death when she's going to do it herself for free?" he asked incredulously. "That would be stupid. As for a life sentence, she's no danger to society anymore. The only person she's going to harm is herself." The last comment Yamaki made overlooked the possibility that the disturbed woman might have more children—and, should she again become deeply depressed, endanger those children.

Some observers thought the sympathy for Fumiko was misplaced. D.A. Comer remarked, "She had absolutely, positively no right to kill the children. I'm an individual and have normal sympathies for her, but I'm also horrified that a woman would walk into the water and kill her children … We're talking about taking the life of another person."

A homicide detective who was called to the beach when the Kimuras were found said, "Nobody seems to remember that two children died. All they remember is the mother and how distressed she was. But how terrible it must have been to be drowned, forcibly drowned. Those children had bruises on them. Somebody just doesn't submit to the pain of drowning."

Some Japanese-Americans were torn about the case. George Narumi, husband of a woman who owned a store in the Little Tokyo section of Los Angeles, told a newspaper reporter that the drownings were "an unforgivable act." His wife Beverly Narumi pointed out that while it may be common, oyako-shinju is "not a thing you're supposed to do."

At least one observer, William Wetherall, a member of the Japan Suicide Prevention Association and journalist who often writes on issues connected with American ethnic minorities, believed that the Japanese background of the defendant was over-emphasized by media in this case.

He pointed out, "Mothers everywhere (and fathers, too) are capable of killing their children, then themselves, when marital, economic, and other problems exceed their ability to cope." He also said that, contrary to Fumiko's assertion that her rescuers had to be Caucasians, people in Japan "are known to stop even strangers from killing themselves."

In the immediate aftermath of his children's deaths, the shocked and distressed Itsuroku rambled about committing suicide. He was briefly hospitalized and placed in protective custody until doctors were convinced that he could be released without trying to harm himself.

When he returned home, he made a shrine for his dead son and daughter on a small coffee table. A photograph of Kazutaka in a black-and-white kimono stood on the table. Beside it were toy cars and trucks and paper planes. There was also a picture of Yuri in a pink dress.

A small private funeral was held in the Little Tokyo district of Los Angeles for the children. Their bodies were cremated. Itsuroku's brother took their ashes to Japan where they were buried with family.

He was also soon regularly visiting his jailed wife, often arriving before daybreak. In his first meeting with his wife after the killings, he said, "Do you need me? I need you." She answered, "Yes." "We will just leave things as they are and we will live a new way in the future," he said.

A reporter asked if he still saw his girlfriend and he answered with an emphatic American slang expression, "No way!"

Did he forgive his wife? "Of course," he answered. He continued with the disturbing statement that he was "envious" that her bond with the children was so powerful that she could hold them while her head was underwater.

He could not return to work in the immediate aftermath of his children's deaths but was also upset at home. "It is so quiet at home, no sounds of children," he said. He spent much time pasting photographs of his children into a scrapbook. He had to take medication to sleep.

The deeply depressed woman who had wanted to die was in the psychiatric unit of the Los Angeles County Jail. Incarcerated, mourning her children, and facing the possibility of imprisonment or execution, she now had to struggle to find a reason to live when her life was more horrible than it had ever been before.

Doctors treated her with anti-depressants and counseling. In a telephone interview, Fumiko said in a weak, shaky voice, "Living is hard and dying is hard. I must try to want to live."

Much of her time was spent writing poems like the following:

A weak woman must not become a strong woman.
A weak woman must have the courage
To accept what she is . . .
A simple woman, that's me.

Probation for the Dual Drownings

Prosecution and defense worked out a plea agreement that showed great leniency to Fumiko. In October 1985, she pled no contest to two counts of voluntary manslaughter. This meant that she could have been sentenced to a maximum of 13 years imprisonment or placed in a mental hospital.

However, on November 21, 1985, Los Angeles County Superior Court Judge Robert W. Thomas sentenced her to a year in jail and five years of probation. The jail sentence was credited with time served and, since she had been in jail for a year, she was immediately free although ordered to continue psychiatric treatment.

Her attorney, Gerald H. Klausner, commented, "The courts can never punish her as much as she punishes herself."

This writer has not been able to uncover more recent information on Fumiko Kimura. It is likely this "weak woman" prefers an obscurity that allows for privacy.

Bibliography

Dolan, Maura. "Two Cultures Collide Over Act of Despair

Mother Facing Charges in Ceremonial Drowning." *Los Angeles Times*. Feb. 24, 1985.

"Fumiko Kimura: Culture and Socialization Case Study." http://pastebin.com/5QBhZ8uZ

"Mother Placed on Probation in 2 Drownings." *Los Angeles Times*. Nov. 21, 1985.

"Mother's Suicide Try Leaves Child Dead." *Los Angeles Times*. Jan. 30, 1985.

Newton, Michael. *Bad Girls Do It!* Loompanics Unlimited. Port Townsend, Washington. 1993.

Nielsen, John. "Activity Center Quietly Tends Roots to Japan." *Los Angeles Times*. May 6, 1985.

Pound, Leslie. "Mother's Tragic Crime Exposes A Culture Gap." *Chicago Tribune*. June 10, 1985.

Rae-Dupree, Janet and Jones, Jack. "Children in Arms Mother's Trek Into Sea Stuns Her Neighbors." *Los Angeles Times*. Jan. 31, 1985.

Rae-Dupree, Janet and Jones, Jack. "Death in the Sea—Neighbors Stunned by Woman's Action." *Los Angeles Times*. Jan. 31, 1985.

Reese, Michael. "A Tragedy in Santa Monica." *Newsweek*. May 5, 1985.

Stewart, Robert W. "Accused Mother Preoccupied by Death Friend of Woman Whose Children Drowned Testifies at Hearing." *Los Angeles Times*. Mar. 29, 1985.

Wetherall, William. "The Trial of Fumiko Kimura." http://members.jcom.home.ne.jp/yosha/yr/suicide/Kimura_trial.

html.

CHAPTER 4

Elizabeth Brownrigg and the Torture-Murder of Mary Clifford

Living in London, England in the mid-18th Century, Elizabeth Brownrigg was an eminently respectable wife, mother, and midwife. She had long been married to successful house-painter and plumber James Brownrigg, and had borne sixteen children.

Drawings of her show a dark-haired, middle-aged woman whose most striking feature was her large, hooked, irregular nose. She also possessed a pursed mouth, strong chin, and thin neck.

The Brownriggs had grown up in Greenwich where they met and married. In the seventh year of their marriage, they moved to London, probably for the greater employment opportunities there. James Brownrigg made enough at his dual occupations to rent a cottage for vacations.

However, as the family grew, its finances were squeezed. By the time Elizabeth gave birth to their sixteenth child, they had to give up the cottage.

Mrs. Brownrigg supplemented the family income by working as a midwife. She became known for her caring and competency and was considered the best midwife in the district. Her services were much sought after so she decided she needed some help in her work and applied for apprentices.

In 1765, authorities at St. Dunstan's Parish placed impoverished 14-year-old Mary Mitchell in the Brownrigg home as an apprentice. Both the placement officers of St. Dunstan's and the girl herself must have thought her lucky for a chance to learn under the esteemed midwife. Learning such an important skill—in an era when large families were the norm and good midwives were in great demand—was often the only way for a lower-class girl to escape poverty without ending up in the brothel.

The first month of Mary Mitchell's apprenticeship passed without incident. Then the busy midwife decided she needed more assistance. Mary Jones, a teenager who had been living in a foundling hospital, joined Mary Mitchell.

Shortly after that, Mrs. Brownrigg's attitude toward both her young wards changed. She was strangely enraged at them, especially Mary Jones. She often ordered Mary Jones to lay across two chairs, tied her down, and then flogged up and down the girl's body with a whip, only stopping because her arm was too tired to raise it again. Then she splashed water across the beaten, bloodied girl. If Jones fainted, Mrs. Brownrigg shoved her head in a pail of water to revive her.

Mrs. Brownrigg beat both girls senseless for the slightest offense. She also forbade them to leave the home and locked them in their rooms at night. However, Jones' room was near a hall leading to a door opening into the street. The door to the hall was locked each evening but on one night, the key was left in the lock and Jones saw her chance.

That morning, she crept softly to that door and stole out into the street. With one eye blinded and her body covered with wounds, she made her way over the narrow cobblestone streets and back to the foundling hospital. The appalled officials had the hospital's lawyer, Mr. Plumbtree, draw up a letter demanding an explanation for the girl's condition. It was sent to the Brownriggs who made no reply. Amazingly, the hospital's hierarchy took no further action. Perhaps they did not want to antagonize a respected family for the sake of a poor orphan.

Their inaction left Mary Mitchell a prisoner and victim in the Brownrigg house and she would remain there, regularly tormented, beaten, and humiliated, for a year. As Leonard

Gribble wrote in Queens of Crime, Mitchell was "dressed in filthy rags, forced to spend long hours in manual toil, and given food that was little better than kitchen scourings" while being "incessantly beaten and mocked."

One day Mitchell escaped from the home but John Brownrigg, one of Elizabeth and James' sons, caught her in the street and dragged her back. Mrs. Brownrigg doubled her torments as punishment.

Mrs. Brownrigg applied to another precinct for another apprentice and a third Mary, 14-year-old Mary Clifford, was put in the Brownrigg home. With Clifford's appearance, the abuse of the apprentices took a particularly humiliating, semi-sexualized turn as both Marys were forced to work naked while Mrs. Brownrigg beat them bloody with brooms, canes and horsewhips. When she got too tired to keep beating them, Mr. Brownrigg or John would take over. Sometimes Mrs. Brownrigg wrapped chains around the girls' necks and nailed one end to a door.

Banished to the Basement

One morning, Mrs. Brownrigg discovered that Mary Clifford had wet her bed. The infuriated midwife banished the girl to the basement each night from then on, forcing her to sleep in the cellar's freezing coal bin. She allowed the victim a bare mattress but permitted no blankets. After a while, Mrs. Brownrigg took away the mattress and replaced it with a sack and some straw. She gave the girl a diet of bread and water.

The starving Clifford broke open a locked cupboard in a search for food but found it empty. Later she broke through some boards searching for water. Mrs. Brownrigg punished these attempts by forcing the malnourished teenager to strip naked, then beating her over the course of the day with the butt-end of a whip.

Mrs. Brownrigg devised a torture in which a girl's hands were tied together with a rope that was slung through a hook in the ceiling so the victim was hoisted off her feet. As the victim swung helplessly, the midwife beat her with a horsewhip.

When she got tired, her son John would take up the whip. On other occasions, Mrs. Brownrigg would grab a girl's face with her fingers and squeeze so violently that blood ran from the victim's eyes.

Both victims were kept naked for days on end while Clifford was forced into the cellar at night, often with her hands still tied and the heavy chain around her neck.

One day an older Brownrigg son ordered Clifford to put up a canopy over a bedstead. The starved, sickly youngster could not do it. Enraged, he beat her viciously until he could no longer lift his arm.

Gribble pointed out the irony that while Mrs. Brownrigg was beating her apprentices, she was also tending to new mothers and babies. "The hand that had grasped the stock of a horsewhip," he wrote, "and the arm that still ached from the blows delivered upon the bleeding back of a fainting girl, sought to bring comfort and ease to another body wracked with pain … The cries of newly born children must have echoed in her ears alternatively with the groans of her lacerated victim[s]."

Odd as it seems, the Brownriggs' home was large enough that they had a lodger during this period. The lodger was a Frenchwoman and Mary Clifford complained to her about the mistreatment she was suffering. The lodger asked Mrs. Brownrigg about Clifford's story. An outraged Mrs. Brownrigg found Clifford and cut her tongue in two with a pair of scissors.

The torturer took to concentrating on Mary Clifford, sometimes beating her five times each day. She would not stop until blood streamed down the girl's body, at which point she ordered the weeping teenager to wash herself in a tub of cold water. Mrs. Brownrigg forced Mary Mitchell to watch as she beat Clifford bloody.

Soon there were signs that gangrene was setting into Clifford's wounds. At about this time, Mary Clifford's stepmother came to the Brownrigg home to inquire after her. James Brownrigg answered the door and said there was no Mary Clifford apprenticed there. The stepmother pressed on, saying she was certain she had been told the young girl was at the Brownrigg home. Mr. Brownrigg brusquely ordered her off his property and threatened to take her before the lord-mayor unless she immediately left and never came back. Then he slammed the door in her face.

Her suspicions aroused, the stepmother went to the house next door and asked if they had heard of Mary Clifford. The family living there was named Deacon and the husband was a baker but he was not at home when Mrs. Clifford called. Mrs. Deacon said that her family had often been alarmed by the sounds of moans and groans from the Brownrigg home. She promised to try to get to the bottom of the matter. As the two women were talking, Mr. Deacon came home. He agreed that the Brownrigg home should be watched.

At this time, Mr. Brownrigg purchased a hog that he put in the covered yard. The yard had a skylight that he removed to allow the animal more air.

With the skylight out of the way, it was easier for others to see into the Brownrigg residence. Mr. Deacon asked his servants to observe the neighbors and try to spot the young apprentices. One day, a maid looking from her window spied a naked teenager lying in the pig's bed. The girl was smeared with blood and pig excrement. The maid called Mrs. Deacon who alerted some men in the area. They dropped bits of dirt down to get the girl's attention.

She looked up but did not say anything. It seemed she might be incapable of speech.

Mrs. Deacon sent for Mary Clifford's stepmother and for the overseers of St. Dunstan's who had placed the girl with Mrs. Brownrigg. The overseer who met up with Mrs. Deacon and Mrs. Clifford was named Mr. Grundy. Mrs. Deacon, Mrs. Clifford, Mr. Grundy, and the maid who had first spotted the pitiful-looking adolescent went to the Brownrigg home and demanded to see Mary Clifford. Again they were told that she was not there. However, Mary Mitchell was brought out to them.

The maid said Mary Mitchell was not the girl she had seen from the window. Grundy sent for a constable and the law officer demanded to look through the house. While James Brownrigg allowed his home to be searched, he also threatened legal action against all the members of the group. Grundy searched but could not find Mary Clifford.

The impromptu semi-posse left, taking Mary Mitchell with them. Mr. Grundy escorted her to a workhouse. There she was helped out of a leather bodice that stuck so tightly to fresh wounds that she shrieked as it was removed.

When the parish overseer asked what had happened to her, the frightened girl asked if she would be sent back to the Brownrigg home. He assured her that she would not be. Finally feeling safe, she spilled out the story of the horrors of the past year. She added that she knew Mary Clifford was still at the Brownrigg home because she had seen her on the stairs just before he and the others knocked on the door.

Grundy and other concerned people returned to the Brownrigg house, determined to make a more thorough search. James Brownrigg sent for a lawyer and threatened to drag them all into court. The overseer summoned a police officer who said he would take Brownrigg to jail unless the girl was produced.

Finally, James Brownrigg reluctantly showed them where Mary Clifford was: squeezed into a cupboard in the dining room. She had bruises and cuts all over her tiny starved body. Mr. Brownrigg was forced onto a coach that took him to jail.

Mrs. Brownrigg and son John returned home to find James Brownrigg and Mary Clifford both gone and realized that their crimes had been discovered. They grabbed their valuables and left the area.

Mary Clifford followed Mary Mitchell to St. Bartholomew's Hospital. The doctors were unable to save Clifford who died a few days later.

The search was on for Elizabeth Brownrigg and her son. The two of them tried to disguise themselves, then headed for the town of Wandsworth, and finally lodged with a shopkeeper named Mr. Dunbar. A few days after they moved in, Mr. Dunbar read a newspaper in which he saw descriptions of a mother and son wanted for murder. The resemblance between the pair wanted by the law and his new lodgers was too exact to be coincidental, he decided. He reported his suspicions to police and a constable went to the shopkeeper's house and arrested the fugitives. Mother and son were put on a carriage to London.

All three Brownriggs were tried at Old Bailey. The news media of the time had a field day with the sensational story of the middle-aged midwife who sadistically tortured young girls. *Gentleman's Magazine* in particular gave the monstrous Brownriggs a lip-smacking treatment worthy of the trashiest of our modern tabloids.

Elizabeth Brownrigg was convicted of murder and sentenced to death. Husband and son were acquitted of murder and remanded to stand trial on lesser charges. Astonishingly, they would each serve only six months in prison for their very willing, active participation in these heinous crimes.

Rev. Silas Told, a clergyman well known as a missionary to the imprisoned, counseled an apparently remorseful Mrs. Brownrigg after her conviction. She confessed her guilt to him and said she agreed with the judgment of the court.

On the morning of her execution, she was allowed a visit with her husband and son. Her son knelt before her and she bent to hug him. Then she and James Brownrigg fell to their knees and prayed. "Dear James," she said, "I beg that God, for Christ's sake, will be reconciled, and that he will not leave me, nor forsake me, in the hour of death and in the day of judgement."

Onlookers shouted abuse at the murderess as she was carted to her death at Tyburn's field. Rev. Told pleaded with the crowd to pray for the penitent doomed woman but they responded with infuriated curses. "The devil will fetch her!" some yelled. "I hope she burns in hell!" others screamed.

As she stood on the gallows, Elizabeth Brownrigg prayed aloud for the salvation of her soul and confessed her guilt.

Her body was taken to Surgeons' Hall for dissecting by interns. Hopefully, she did some good in death by serving as a teaching tool for future physicians. Later, her skeleton was hung up in Surgeons' Hall.

Today, a statue of Elizabeth Brownrigg graces the "Wicked Women" exhibit at the London Dungeon, a famous British horror museum.

The Baniszewski Echo

Elizabeth Brownrigg's crimes inspired those of Sarah Metyard, a London woman who was executed for similar offenses within a year of Mrs. Brownrigg. A daughter assisted Metyard in beating and torturing female apprentices. Both women were executed at Tyburn and their skeletons exhibited at Surgeons' Hall.

The Elizabeth Brownrigg incident has an even more bizarre 20th Century echo in the story of Gertrude Baniszewski, torture-slayer of Sylvia Likens. The latter case took place in 1965. Carnival workers Lester and Betty Likens left two of their daughters, 14-year-old disabled Jenny and pretty, lively 15-year-old Sylvia, to board with Gertrude Baniszewski (pronounced Ban-i-shef-ski).

There are a startling number of parallels between the Elizabeth Brownrigg case and that of Gertrude Baniszewski. Like Mrs. Brownrigg, Gertrude was the mother of a large family (seven children). She also started beating Sylvia soon after the girls began living with her. Just as Mrs. Brownrigg concentrated on Mary Clifford, Baniszewski concentrated on Sylvia. However, the Baniszewski case was more extreme in this regard with Jenny being beaten only a few times although she was threatened with the same tortures inflicted on Sylvia if she tried to get help for her sister.

Like Mary Mitchell with Mary Clifford, Jenny was forced to watch while Sylvia was abused. Son John and husband James assisted Mrs. Brownrigg in abusing her charges. Gertrude's children and neighborhood youngsters joined in the beating and torture of Sylvia. Mrs. Brownrigg ordered Mary Clifford to spend nights in the basement after wetting her bed and Gertrude consigned Sylvia to her basement after a bedwetting incident. Like the midwife's victims, Sylvia often had her arms tied together and was hung from a hook. The apprentices had their heads dunked into pails of water and a bound Sylvia was forced into scalding baths. Like the hapless Marys, Sylvia was starved and often forced to appear naked in front of her tormentors.

In both cases, neighbors who "didn't want to get involved" ignored the evidence of abuse in their midst and authorities did too little too late when they did get reports of violence.

Finally, in both instances the adult woman behind the horror was punished severely while her accomplices got off relatively easily. Gertrude Baniszewski served twenty years in prison before being paroled over fierce public opposition. Her 17-year-old daughter Paula, who beat Sylvia unmercifully and rubbed salt into the girl's wounds, served about seven years in prison. Three male accomplices, all minors, spent only eighteen months in detention.

None of this means that Baniszewski knew anything about the earlier case. Unlike Sarah Metyard, who is believed to have deliberately patterned her crimes after those of Brownrigg, it is unlikely Baniszewski ever heard of her torturous foremother. Rather, it indicates that the motives of the two murderers were probably similar. Both were middle-aged women who may have been jealous of girls in the bloom of youth who possessed the sexual attractiveness they themselves had lost. It is also likely that both viewed their young charges as sexually "immoral." It is known that Baniszewski considered Sylvia incorrigibly promiscuous; a few days before the girl's death, she prodded an accomplice into burning the words "I'm a prostitute and proud of it!" into her flesh with a hot sewing needle. Brownrigg may have thought her apprentices "fallen women" since that was so commonly the fate of impoverished young females of the era.

Why did bed-wetting provoke such wrath in both these killers? Kate Millett speculated in fictional passages of *The Basement*, her book about the Gertrude Baniszewski case, that Baniszewski may have associated bedwetting with that urinary incontinence that sometimes accompanies enthusiastic sex or perhaps the g-spot "squirting" that some women do.

This speculation is not unreasonable and such a link may have been behind either or both women's overheated reactions to bedwetting. Another possibility is that, as mothers of large families, they bitterly resented having to spend so much of their lives cleaning up bodily discharges by changing a seemingly endless cycle of diapers. Monstrous as both these women were, they probably loved their own children enough to suppress this rage with them. But they had no such emotional bond with other people's children. Thus, they may have vented a lifetime of pent-up fury at having to do so much "dirty work" in their cruel punishment of their bedwetting charges.

Perhaps the most ominous parallel in the cases is the failure of others to intervene in time. Two centuries had not altered the reluctance of neighbors to report the evidence of abuse that they saw and heard. Nor had it ensured that authorities informed of possible child abuse would act strongly and swiftly enough to save the lives of cruelly mistreated young people.

Bibliography

http://www.hauntedattraction.com/29/coverstory29.html

http://www.ihrinfo.ac.uk/reviews/paper/pooleyj.html

http://www.exclassics.org/newgate/ng311.htm, The Newgate Calendar, vol. 2, 1825.

Dean, John. *The Indiana Torture Slaying.* Borf Books, Brownsville, KY, 1999.

Everitt, David. *Human Monsters.* Contemporary Books, Chicago, IL, 1993.

Gribble, Leonard R. *Queens of Crime.* Hurst & Blackett, Ltd., London, England. 1932.

Millett, Kate. *The Basement*. Simon and Schuster. New York, NY. 1979.

CHAPTER 5

The Torment and Tragedy of Johnathan James

For a child who had watched his fraternal twin brother die as the result of abuse only a month before talking to reporters, 10-year-old Joseph James seemed remarkably composed albeit understandably sad as he spoke to reporters in August 2011. "I wanted to help him but I didn't do nothing because I would get in trouble, too," Joseph plaintively recalled.

Joseph's fraternal twin, Johnathan James, was killed in July 2011 while the two boys visited their father, Michael Ray James, and stepmother Tina Alberson. Prior to this court-ordered visit, an anxious Johnathan had telephoned his grandmother Sue Shotwell. "Can I come to your house instead?" Johnathan asked. "I know I'm going to be in trouble while I'm there because I always am."

Shotwell told him he would have to visit his father and stepmother. She later said she had no idea how harshly the father and stepmother had been disciplining the boy.

The visit took place in the Redbird community section of Dallas, Texas. Both Alberson and James are dark-haired and extremely obese. James sports a ragged beard growth. Alberson's photographs show an unusual amount of facial hair growth for a female that gives the appearance of what is often called a "five o'clock shadow."

Joseph and Johnathan were blond-haired and Johnathan was chubby.

Deprival of Water as Punishment for Bedwetting

During the visit, Johnathan was accused of stealing guitar strings from Joseph. Johnathan also wet the bed.

Law enforcement investigators believe that Alberson and James punished the boy by refusing to allow him to drink water or any other liquid for five days. A tape-recorded interrogation of Alberson in the immediate aftermath of the 2011 death revealed that she admitted using the deprivation of liquids as a punishment.

On the recording, Alberson, then 43, says in apparent confusion, "I obviously did this. I didn't mean to do this." During that interrogation, Alberson frequently contradicted herself, stating that Johnathan did have access to water but that she did not watch to see if he drank it. She gives no explanation as to why he might abstain on his own from liquids. At other times, she admitted withholding liquids from him. She told officers, "He always said he was thirsty. He was in time out, and every two minutes he would say, 'I need a drink … I need to go to the bathroom.'"

Law enforcement officers believe that while denied water and suffering terrible thirst, Johnathan was forced to stand in a spot in the kitchen that had no air conditioning while July temperatures in that Texas neighborhood climbed to over 100 degrees. As the thirsty boy stood, he was forced to hold a sack of potatoes over his head. Joseph James described this punishment as follows: "They made him stand in front of a window. They put an 'X' on the floor and an 'X' on the window and the sun was coming straight through it and there was no air conditioning there."

Joseph remembered that during the five days in which he was denied liquids, Johnathan sometimes pretended he had to use the toilet so Albertson and James would let him visit the bathroom where he would attempt to drink water straight from the faucet. Joseph said Johnathan had gone without liquids for five days when his stepmother and father gave him a peanut butter and jelly sandwich. "The peanut butter got stuck in his throat and they still wouldn't let him have water," Joseph said.

Later that same day, Johnathan collapsed. Joseph recalled, "When we picked him up and leaned him over the kitchen chair he was shaking and moaning."

Dehydration and the Bathtub Treatment

Police documents report, "A child of his age would exhibit progressive symptoms of his dehydration, including complaining of thirst, progressively becoming lethargic, appearing dry (cracked lips, sunken eyes), mental status changes, decreased urine output and eventually shock/cardiac arrest."

After Johnathan collapsed, Alberson and James put him in a bathtub. They ran cold water, apparently believing that would help lower his temperature and bring him back to consciousness. When they saw that the bath was not helping, they drove him to the Methodist Charlton Medical Center—where his grandmother Sue Shotwell works as an administrator.

Alberson told hospital personnel that her stepson was sick. Suspecting abuse, hospital workers called police even as other workers struggled to revive Johnathan.

Hospital employees informed Shotwell that her grandson was at the hospital in which she worked. She rushed to his side. Shocked to see the normally outgoing and active child unconscious and with his breathing frighteningly slowed, she leaned close to the boy and whispered in his ear, "I love you."

Shortly after his death, Johnathan's mother Krista Bishop commented sadly, "It should never have happened." She recalled seeing him unconscious. "He was pale, not life to him, nothing," she said. "He was just lying there … it was just heartbreaking." After medical personnel tried for two hours to revive Johnathan, a heartbroken Krista Bishop gave them permission to stop trying.

Prior to suffering abuse, Johnathan was a healthy and outgoing child. Some of his favorite activities were riding a bicycle, swimming, and participating with his brother in Cub Scouts. Grandmother Sue Shotwell remembers Johnathan as an energetic youngster.

"He was very tan from being outside," she said. "He could run out the door and I'd hand him a bottle of water like he was running a marathon." She also described him as a friendly, cheerful child who never held a grudge.

She recalled, "Johnathan could forgive you no matter what you did. You could ground him and he would say, 'I love you, Mimi.'" He and his brother Joseph were close. At school, the twins often played together at recess. They received good grades and were honored as "Students of the Month" during the same time period.

Both Alberson and James were charged with first-degree felony injury to a child. They are being tried separately. Alberson's trial took place first.

On January 17, 2013, Michael Ray James testified against his wife in a Dallas, Texas courtroom.

"I felt like she was the one responsible for him ending up the way he did," James said. He also testified that on their way to the hospital, "I flat out told her that if anything happens to my son, I'll never forgive her." *Huff Post Crime* reports, "James has significant health problems and is legally blind. He said in court that he didn't know the extent of his son's suffering."

The prosecution played the tape recording of the interrogation in which Alberson admitted withholding liquids from Johnathan but also said, "I didn't mean to do this."

A medical examiner testified that there was not a drop of urine in Johnathan's bladder when he died due to liquid deprivation.

Joseph James testified to seeing his brother deprived of water and being too afraid of his father and stepmother to sneak it to him.

Alberson took the stand in her own defense. She testified that she sometimes limited Johnathan's water intake for brief periods when he misbehaved but that she had not deprived him of it for days. She testified that she had seen him drinking water during the days before his death and that she had not seen him appearing sickly until just before taking him to the hospital.

On January 18, 2013, Tina Alberson was found guilty of reckless injury to a child, a second-degree felony that is less than the first-degree felony injury to a child of which prosecutors had hoped to convict her. Usually, the possible sentence range for reckless injury to a child is between five to twenty years in prison. However, since Alberson was convicted in 2001 of aggravated assault with a deadly weapon, the possible sentence range for her on this new conviction was from five years to life imprisonment.

During the sentencing phase, Shotwell testified to how Johnathan disliked visiting his father and stepmother and could not understand why he was always getting into trouble at that home. She elaborated, "There was a time he came home with a red mark around his neck and we asked him what happened and he said, 'Tina.'"

The judge sentenced Alberson to 85 years in prison on January 22. She showed no reaction as sentence was pronounced. After the sentence was passed, Shotwell made a statement to the court in which she talked directly to Alberson. Shotwell said, "We trusted you with our baby. If I could speak for Johnathan right now, I would know—you would know – that he still loves you."

Talking to reporters outside the courtroom, Krista Bishop indicated she was pleased by the sentence. "We got what we needed," she commented.

Alberson will not be able to even apply for parole until she has served one-quarter of her sentence or a little more than twenty years. Bill Fay, an attorney for Alberson, said he will appeal but would not specify the grounds for that appeal.

Commenting on this case, CNN anchor Brook Baldwin called Johnathan's "a totally preventable death" and observed, "Adults failed Johnathan James."

Sue Shotwell expressed skepticism about Michael Ray James's claim that he was not responsible for his son's death. "He could've stopped it," she asserted, "What person in their right mind deprives anyone of water?"

It remains to be seen whether or not a jury and judge will hold James legally accountable for Johnathan's agony and death.

Bibliography

"Jonathan James, 10, Dies From Dehydration After Dallas Parents Deprive Him Of Water For 5 Days." *Huff Post Impact.* August 31, 2011.

Kotz, Pete. "Jonathan James, 10, Dies of Dehydration After Being Denied Water for Wetting Bed." *True Crime Report.* August 29, 2011.

McLaughlin, Michael. "Tina Alberson Admist She Withheld Water From Stepson Jonathan James, Who Died From Dehydration." *Huff Post Crime.* January 17, 2013.

McLaughlin, Michael. "Tina Alberson Guilty Of Causing Johnathan James' Dehydration Death." *Huff Post Crime.* January 19, 2013.

Merchant, Norman. "Tina Marie Alberson, Stepmom, Gets 85 Years in Dehydration Death Of Jonathan James." *Huff Post Crime.* January 22, 2013.

Nielsen, Jon. "Boy who died of dehydration was punished for wetting bed." *The Dallas Morning News.* August 26, 2011.

Piper, Brandie. "Jonathan James dies from dehydration punishment." KSDK.com. Aug. 26, 2011.

CHAPTER 6

The "Handcuff Man" and His Victims

For two decades, a man operating variously in Atlanta, Georgia and Tampa, Florida, preyed on gay male prostitutes and men he wrongly believed were homosexual prostitutes. The attacks are believed to have started in 1968. A hustler would meet a dark-haired, thin, bespectacled John with bushy eyebrows. Sometimes he wore an expensive suit; other times he was casually attired in jeans and T-shirt. Sometimes he sported a mustache or beard. If shaven, he always seemed to have a heavy five o'clock shadow.

This John paid the prostitute merely to take a drink of vodka which must have struck the hired man as an unusually easy way to earn a few dollars. The well-spoken man might tell the hustler that a study was being conducted on the effects of drinking a certain amount of alcohol so he asked the fellow to participate in this "research" for $50 or $100. Whatever the ruse, the drink was spiked and the prostitute (or presumed prostitute) quickly lost consciousness.

The victim awoke to a horror. Often he found himself handcuffed and burned on his genitals or legs. Sometimes the attacker put cigarettes out on the victim, other times he doused the victim with flammable liquids and lit him on fire.

Victims were reluctant to press charges. After all, most were prostitutes and, as a result, fearful and distrustful of police. They often did not want family and relatives to know of their occupation. They also might not have been "out" to their families about their own homosexuality or bisexuality. Frequently troubled and "on the margins" individuals to begin with, they were typically left to cope with the psychological and physical devastation of these horrendous attacked without even the compensation of justice being done to the victimizer.

To Print Or Not To Print

The air in the newsroom of *The Atlanta Journal Constitution,* the city's biggest newspaper, was thick with tension. It was the newspaper's tradition to withhold the name of a suspect in a criminal investigation who was neither a fugitive nor officially charged with a crime. Did they dare break with tradition in the case of the Handcuff Man?

As reporter Richard Greer noted, the name of Robert Lee Bennett Jr. was "meaningless to most Atlantans, his right to privacy as great as any other little-known person's." What if Bennett was not the Handcuff Man? By publishing his name, would the newspaper be invading his privacy? Would it be subjecting an innocent man to unwarranted public notoriety? Some feared such a move would compromise the privacy of innocent citizens in the future. Because of this concern, previous stories on the Handcuff Man had not only refrained from mentioning his name but had left out information that might lead readers to identify him.

However, some in the newsroom argued that public safety was at stake. They pointed out that there were many documents connecting the wealthy local attorney to the Handcuff Man's cruel crimes against gay hustlers. Bennett had been arrested for kidnapping an undercover officer posing as a hustler. When his ex-wife sued him for divorce, her lawyer and several men had accused him of being the Handcuff Man. And, as Greer wrote, "State archives contained more than 400 pages of documents providing solid links between Bennett and the sadistic acts of the Handcuff Man."

Editors at *The Atlanta Journal Constitution* still were not satisfied that publicly naming him as the suspected torturer was justified. Then his most recent victim picked his photograph out of a group of photos. And a victim of years previous also fingered him. That did it.

The Atlanta Journal Constitution ran a story naming Robert Lee Bennett Jr. as the suspected Handcuff Man.

The next day, Tampa police requested information from their Atlanta counterparts and the latter charged Bennet with an attack on a Florida man who had been doused in gasoline and lit on fire. The victim has survived but the injuries were so severe that both of his legs had to be amputated.

"In retrospect I have no doubts," Greer later said. "Considering the information we had by the time we published Bennett's name, our natural fears should have been allayed. Our prime concern should have been prodding the police to enhance the safety of the young men who were at risk."

Robert Lee Bennett Jr. was 22 months old when he was adopted. Prior to the adoption, had the infant been abused, neglected, or traumatized in a way that might have contributed to a warped psyche? The answer is not known.

The previously childless couple who became parents when they brought baby Robert into their home consisted of a successful attorney, Robert Bennett, and a homemaker, Annabelle Maxwell Bennett. They had married in 1993 and set up housekeeping in Towanda, Pennsylvania. In 1943, the elder Robert Bennett was appointed president of Citizen and Northern Bank. Annabelle Bennett volunteered for the Red Cross and Robert Bennett was a frequent fundraiser for the Boy Scouts. The family of three did a great deal of vacation traveling.

"Bob" Bennett Jr. does not appear to fit the profile of a serial predator. The background of a vicious criminal is frequently one of severe deprivation, either economic or psychological or both. In many cases, there is a background of physical or sexual abuse or emotional abuse by unstable, repressed, neurotic, superstitious, or alcoholic parents. None of this is known to have occurred to Bennett.

Both parents appear to have loved him and are believed to

have been close to him. As a child, Bobby was a Boy Scout and had a paper route. "If the weather was inclement, his father would drive him around in his Fleetwood Cadillac to deliver newspapers," recalled Leon Wizelman, a friend of the family who, as a car dealer, sold them cars. "Both parents were very high-class people."

The adolescent Bob is remembered as an outgoing teenager, involved in many organizations. Never an athlete, he was not among the most popular boys in school but neither was he the victim of bullying. He belonged to the Glee Club, the chorus, was features editor of the student newspaper, and was a member of the science club. He appears to have had a lifelong love for botany. *The Atlanta Journal Constitution* reported, "He won second place in a science fair for a project about orchids."

For his high school graduation, Bob's father gave him a picturesque $167,000 cottage located by Lake Wesauking.

Bennett appeared to have grown into a bright and accomplished young man. He graduated from the University of Denver in 1969 and went on to earn a master's degree in political science from the University of Virginia. However, in 1971, while studying there, he was charged with indecent exposure. Records about this case have been expunged.

In 1974, Bennett received his law degree from Atlanta's Emory University, took a job with his father's law firm of Davis, Murphy, and Bennett in Pennsylvania, and had another run-in with the law. According to the Atlanta Journal Constitution, Bennett allegedly observed a "plainclothes Atlanta officer who was working undercover to catch male hustlers on Fifth Street near Cypress Street." Although the article does not report how successful the officer was at arresting male prostitutes, he was apparently quite good at imitating them since Bennett mistook him for one and kidnapped him. The undercover cop was soon rescued, uninjured, by backup police officers.

Kidnapping charges had been dropped by the time Bennett came to trial. His attorney cut an excellent deal by which Bob pleaded no contest to the relatively minor offense of simple battery. The millionaire lawyer got off with a meager $75 fine.

In 1976, Bennett had another legal difficulty, and one that led him to move away from Towanda. A young New Yorker was traveling in Pennsylvania when, police believe, he met up with Bob Bennett. The attorney paid the man to drink, and the two had sex in Bennett's car. They then headed for the lakeside cottage that had been Bennett's high school graduation gift.

For some reason, the man from New York got scared. He grabbed Bennett's keys, jumped in the lawyer's car, and drove off. He quickly crashed the Bennett's car.

The man refused to cooperate with police. Apparently, like so many of Bennett's victims, he wanted to keep his encounter with Bennett private. Also, according to an article in *The Atlanta Journal Constitution*, a Towanda police officer claimed that another officer "discouraged the alleged victim from pushing an investigation." Lindsay speculated that the officer did this because Robert Bennett Sr. "held a seat on the Civil Service Board, which reviews police promotions." Another investigator seconded that opinion. "Nobody wanted to press charges against him because of the influence of his father," the investigator said. "His father was gold."

Guy Notte, an Atlanta lawyer who would eventually handle both divorce and criminal matters for Bob Bennett Jr., recalled a conversation he once had with a saddened Bennett Sr. about his son. "He is my cross to bear," the father said. "My wife loves him dearly and I love my wife and that's the only reason I put up with him."

The Towanda police were, however, able to persuade Bennett Jr. that it would be best for him if he left the area. He moved to Atlanta.

Troubled Marriage

The attorney soon found employment with the Atlanta firm of Kidd, Pickens, and Tate. When not working at his chosen vocation, he was apparently pursuing other, crueler interests.

One victim, James Crowe, later described his frightening encounter with the Handcuff Man. Crowe was just 19 years old. "In the early part of the summer of 1977," he testified in a deposition. "I was on Buford highway and I hitchhiking to Atlanta." Friends had told Crowe that gay men hung out in Piedmont Park so that was where the slender, longhaired youth went.

At Piedmont Park he met a slender, tall fellow wearing large glasses.

"Do you drink?" the man asked.

"Yeah," Crowe responded.

"Want to make some money?"

"How?"

The man told Crowe that all he had to do was drink. "The more shots you drink, the more money I'll give you," the man explained.

Crowe stepped into the tall man's blue Cadillac. The older man gave his new friend some liquor and Crowe was soon feeling tipsy. The man drove to a trailer park and began playing with Crowe's penis.

Suddenly Crowe sensed something wrong. He tried to get out of the car but the other man grabbed Crowe's long hair and pulled hard. Still Crowe unlocked the car door and torpedoed out. As he did so, he felt a sharp, stinging pain on his right shoulder. He ran. His attacked ran after him. Crowe stumbled and fell, then got up and started screaming and throwing rocks at his assailant. Crowe escaped but did not seek medical attention for his wounds or report the attack to the police. He gave as his reasons that he does not "like doctors" and did not want his sister to know he hustled.

A couple of weeks later, Crowe was back at Piedmont Park, this time accompanied by another, more experienced homosexual prostitute who was, in Crowe's words, "trying to show me some ropes." Crowe spotted the attacker who had plied him with a drug-laced drink and stabbed his shoulder. He pointed the man out to the other hustler who recognized the thin, dark-haired man. "He's got a bad reputation," Crowe's comrade related. "They call him Handcuff Man."

During roughly this same time period, Bennett, at age 29, began dating a female secretary, Sandra Powell, who worked at the law firm. She was five years older than Bennett and earned $17,000 a year. They shared rides home from work, then started formally dating. Bennett proposed to her in 1978 and Powell accepted. She agreed to marry him despite his honest admission to her that they would not be husband and wife in the complete sense. Bennett told her that he was impotent.

"The marriage was one of convenience for both parties," Guy Notte observed. "They enjoyed each other's company and he treated her like a princess."

Did Bennett's bride see anything in him besides dollar signs? Maybe. "He was an intelligent man," Notte said. "He had a very dry sense of humor at times."

Shortly after Bennett married, he quite the law firm and got a job as a jewelry salesman at Davison's department store in Columbia Mall. Then, for reasons unknown, he stopped working. He did not need money. His father had died of heart failure and left his son a great deal of money, including a portfolio of stocks, hundreds of thousands of dollars, and the Bennett's elegant Towanda mansion.

According to Sandra Powell Bennett's testimony at their divorce trial, quitting paid work did not lead to his becoming much of a househusband. "He would just hand around the house all day and he would be in his robe when I got home," she stated. She elaborated that she continued to work at her paid job and then did all the cooking and housecleaning when she returned home. Bennett often suffered insomnia. The main pleasures in his life appeared to be working in his garden and painting landscapes. The situation was "very stressful" for her, she recalled, but she "kept it inside and tried not to let it affect the relationship." Despite their troubles, they discussed adopting a child but never followed through with action.

During his marriage, it is believed Bennett pursued a hobby in addition to gardening and painting—torture. His confused and lonely wife apparently knew nothing about his brutal practices.

In early 1982, young Cleveland Bubb was standing on an Atlanta street corner. Bubb was a handsome youth with a rather wide nose and an oval face. A man in a blue car drove up to Bubb. "Would you drink a bottle of vodka with me?" the driver asked. "I'll give you $100 to do it." Bubb got in the car and the two drank together. The man wore expensive clothes but appeared somewhat sloppy. He had a gold chain around his neck and the first three buttons of his shirt open. After drinking in the car, they went to a bar with the name The Texas Drilling Company and downed a few more.

The next thing Bubb remembers is awakening in the a parking lot wearing only his "parachute pants." He suffered two cigarette burns, one on his stomach and another on an arm. Later Bubb would say he wished he could "take a bottle and break it over [his attacker's] fucking head."

In September 1982, something happened that shocked Sandra Powell Bennett to the core and led her to separate from her husband.

Bob Bennett Jr. was arrested for murder and armed robbery. His wife was walking home from a bus stop when she saw her handcuffed husband being led from their home by uniformed police officers.

"What is it?" she gasped. "What have you done?"

"I don't know," he replied, seemingly as baffled as she was. "They won't tell me anything."

Bennett was charged with the murder of James Lee Johnson, 24, a dishwasher who had been shot and whose body was found with his wallet missing.

Although the charges were dropped two months later because of insufficient evidence, Sandra Bennett did not return to her husband. He contested her suit for divorce. According to Notte, his lawyer, "He knew she was going to get out of the marriage but he contested it simply because of the money, because she wanted a fortune."

Three gay male prostitutes testified at the divorce trial that they believed Bennett to be the notorious Handcuff Man. Sandra Bennett was granted a divorce and awarded a $40,00 settlement. Additionally, the court ordered Bennett to pay $12,000 in lawyers' fees.

1985: Attack on Max Shrader

In the years following his divorce, Bob Bennett divided his time between Atlanta and Florida where he stayed with his disabled mother in winter and spring. Annabelle Bennett had been in a bad car accident while vacationing in Kenya and had been left paralyzed as a result. Her major comfort was the devoted son who doted on her as she had doted on him while he was growing up. He spent much time comforting his mother and keeping her company but Bennett "could be verbally abusive to both his father and his mother," Notte remembered. An acquaintance of the Bennetts recalled that Bob Bennett "made comments sometimes that she could irritate him to the point he wanted to scream. We said, 'Bob, you probably do a lot of things to make her scream.'"

In 1983, Bennett was banned from the Gallus, an Atlanta bar and restaurant with a predominantly gay clientele. The ban came about when a gay male prostitute complained to Sergeant J. D. Kirkland that Bennett was known to pick hustlers up and injure them. On November 1983, Bennett signed a document saying he understood he had "been barred from the premises of the Gallus restaurant" and that he could "be arrested without further notice and charged with Criminal Trespass" if he returned to it.

In 1984, a young man named Myers Von Hirschsprung was standing on a street corner near his home, waiting for a bus to take him downtown. A car approached him.

"Need a ride?" the driver asked.

The youth did. He got in the car and exchanged introductions and pleasantries with the middle-aged man behind the wheel.

"I'm a professor at Georgia Tech," the driver told Von Hirschsprung. As Myers recalled, the man's speech had a rather slow cadence to it. "I'm doing a study about people's drinking and their tolerance levels for it. I'll pay you $100 to drink whatever kind of liquor you want to, Myers if you'll drink it as quickly as you can. We'll go somewhere and you'll drink and then walk and if you're walking okay, you'll drink some more."

Von Hirschsprung was instantly suspicious. They were near Von Hirschsprung's destination and he decided he would not try to earn $100 from this stranger. "Please just let me out," he told the supposed professor.

The stranger allowed Von Hirschsprung to exit the car.

It was 1985 and a gay male prostitute who used the nickname "Chico" was picked up in Atlanta by a dark-haired, bespectacled customer. As the man drove, he showed Chico a pair of handcuffs and urged, "Try them on. I just want to see how they look on you."

Chico was wary. "Please stop the car," he said.

"No," was the ominous reply.

Chico realized that the door lock had been removed and the handle covered with duct tape. However, the window was open and Chico was a small man. Terrified, Chico dove out the window as the car was moving.

The fall left Chico badly bruised and scratched but otherwise uninjured.

Others were not as fortunate.

Max Shrader was a handsome and streetwise Atlanta youth who sported small black tattoos on both forearms. One sunny day in April 1985, he was hanging around the streets of Ponce de Leon and Barnett and, in his own words, "looking for some money," when he spotted a potential source.

A man in a car kept driving around the block. The man parked at a curb and motioned for Shrader to approach.

"Get a hard-on for me," the driver said. "I'll drive around the block and come back." True to his word, he took off and circled back to the same place. "Would you like a drink of vodka?" he asked Shrader.

"Yeah," the hustler replied.

Still behind the wheel of his car with Shrader standing on the street, the customer handed Shrader a brown-colored drink.

"I mixed some coke in it," the man said.

Shrader began drinking. Almost immediately he felt woozy, then crumpled to the ground. He knew the drink had been laced with something. In a semi-conscious state, Shrader was pulled into the passenger seat of the John's car.

"Don't hurt me!" Shrader screamed.

The driver hit the gas and drove to a wooded area. There he pulled Shrader out of the vehicle. The man took Shrader's clothes off and poured a cold liquid over the youth's genitals. Then the man set Max Shrader's genitals on fire!

The helpless and burning Shrader lay shrieking in agony on the ground as the attacker sped away.

Someone heard Shrader's cries and called police.

Shrader spent two months in the hospital, in terrible pain and often heavily sedated. He could not walk during much of his hospitalization and had to wear a diaper-like gauze over his genital area.

But the Handcuff Man had not satisfied his cruel desires. On June 10, 1986, two Atlanta buddies, Michael Johnson and Anthony "Tony" Poppillia, were hanging out on Ponce De Leon between the Goofy Gofer and the Pegasus. Poppilia was wearing a tight blue fishnet tank top, blue jeans, cowboy boots, and a black hat.

A man driving a car called to Poppilia and Poppilia approached him. The driver introduced himself as "Jim" and asked if Poppilia wished to earn $50 by participating in an Emory University study on the effects of given amounts of alcohol. Poppilia asked Jim to wait.

Then Poppilia ran back to his friend Michael Johnson. The pals usually gave each other descriptions of guys who picked them up and the license plates of cars when picked up by men who were driving. Poppilia did that this time. Poppilia related that he was going to drink some alcohol for this "researcher" and then find out if he could still walk a straight line. "You can do that if you want to but remember you've got to be at work tomorrow at seven," Johnson said. He also warned Poppilia to be careful because there was a weirdo around attacking guys.

Jim drove Poppilia around, serving him vodka. Eventually, Jim stopped his car behind the Texas Drilling Company bar. "Would you like to put on a pair of shorts so you'll be more comfortable?" Jim asked, holding a pair of cut-off jeans.

Poppilia agreed. Underneath the emergency stairs of the bar, Poppilia peeled off his pants and put on the shorts. The shorts lacked pockets, so he had to leave his wallet and other personal items in his own pants.

The two men went into the bar where they downed a few drinks. Poppilia's memory of the night is fuzzy after that. He recalled that, when they left the bar, Jim seemed to want to get away from him but Poppilia followed him to the car because he needed his pants and the wallet in a pocket. Poppilia got into the passenger seat but them Jim took off and pushed Poppilia out of the vehicle while it was moving.

Poppilia saw a man nearby who carried a garbage can. Poppilia called to the man, who approached. "I just got mugged," Poppilia explained before losing consciousness. He wore only his undershorts and he had suffered several abrasions and bruises. He was later unable to recall removing his shirt of the shorts he had been loaned.

When Poppilia regained consciousness, he saw three men.

"Where are you living?" one of the three asked.

Poppilia gave his address and directions to it. Then he again lost consciousness. He awoke in a Dunkin' Donuts, looking at two Atlanta police officers. "Could you identify the man who called himself 'Jim'?" one cop inquired.

"Yes," Poppilia answered.

He did not have to wait long for "Jim" was standing in the parking lot of the donut shop. Two men who had been alerted to the crime blacked his car with their own vehicles. One of the men was Poppilia's friend, Charles Fallow, who had once been mugged by "Jim." About nine months earlier, Fallow related to authorities, the two of them had shared drinks and the man had handcuffed Fallow before beating and robbing him.

Closing In

Gary Clapp was unemployed in February 1991. Trained as a carpenter, engaged to marry a woman, and the father of a three-year-old daughter, Clapp had left his Massachusetts home for Florida on a quest for employment.

Needing a free meal one evening, Clapp waited outside a Salvation Army office in Tampa. He did not know that the area was frequented by gay male prostitutes and their clients. As Clapp waited, a man drove up in a white Lincoln Town Car and beckoned to Clapp. The thin, dark-haired driver wore a Fu Manchu-style mustache and large, gold-rimmed glasses. He offered Clapp $50 to drink vodka as part of an experiment. "He was well-spoken," Clapp recalled. "He seemed like he was on the up and up. I asked him his name but he wouldn't tell me." Clapp got into the car and settled against the brown leather of the passenger seat. The unemployed man accepted several shots of vodka from a plastic cup as the two men conversed and shared cigarettes. The man had a notebook and pen with him. He jotted down notes as Clapp guzzled drinks.

"You need to drink faster," the "researcher" told Clapp – whose consciousness began getting fuzzy. He has said that he may have visited a bar with the stranger but was not certain. He did not remember the horrendous events that transpired.

A police officer driving on Tampa's Courtney Campbell Causeway spotted what looked like an out-of-control bonfire in a field. He stopped to investigate.

It was the burning body of Gary Clapp.

"I was surprised he lived," firefighter Nelson Garcia III later testified. "We really didn't think he was going to make it."

Clapp's burn injuries were so bad that both his legs had to be amputated above the knee. After his recovery, his fiancée broke off their engagement. Sitting in a wheelchair in a state-run boarding home, a despairing Clapp said, "Things fell apart when this happened. I don't know why the guy didn't just finish me off. This is not going to be easy."

When the cops spread a group of photographs before Clapp, he instantly recognized his attacker. "It took me a minute to say something," Clapp remembered. "I couldn't believe they got him so quick, and seeing his face again, I went into shock."

However, police did not catch Bennett then and he often

returned to Atlanta. In May 1991, a young man named Michael Jordan Jr. was found severely burned.

Jordan was handsome and slightly built with wavy dark hair. He sported a small beard and mustache. He was walking down an Atlanta street when he saw the motioning of a man in a white Lincoln. Jordan noticed that the man's car tag said, "Pinellas County, Florida." Being from Florida himself, Jordan asked if he was from Clearwater.

"No, I'm from St. Pete," the smiling driver replied. "Do you want to make $50?"

"Well, what do I got to do to make $50?" Jordan asked.

"All you got to do is drink," the man informed him. "I got three pints and, if you drink it all, I'll give you $50."

"Drink, that's it? Sure."

"First, walk around the corner to Fifth Street and Juniper," the driver instructed. "Then take your shirt off."

Jordan headed for Fifth and Juniper but did not remove his shirt when he got there. The Lincoln tailed him, then went to a nearby parking lot. Again the stranger motioned for Jordan, who went to the parking lot and got in the car with the older man. Jordan took his shirt off and the driver gave him a drink.

"You got a problem here," Jordan cheerfully informed him. "I come from a long line of alcoholics and I'm going to be able to drink this with no problem."

"If you get a bit drunk, don't worry," the man assured Jordan. "I'll rent you a room and you'll be all right." Then he asked Jordan to take his penis out and try to get it hard. Jordan complied with that request as well. The stranger told Jordan that he was going to go to the store for a Coca Cola to mix in the drinks. He handed the youth a $20 bill and Jordan stuck it in his moccasins, then sat down in the parking lot and waited for the man to return.

When the fellow returned, he gave Jordan another drink.

And there Jordan's memory ends until he woke up in a hospital in agony because of the terrible burns over his genitals, buttocks, and legs.

Jordan had been naked and unconscious when his assailant dropped him on the street behind an Atlanta hotel. Authorities could not interview the badly injured man in the immediate aftermath of the crime because he was either in excruciating agony or heavily medicated.

Special fears haunted Jordan because of where he had been wounded. "If I get an erection, it bleeds and they don't know if I'm going to be normal again there," he said from his hospital bed.

May 1991 was apparently a busy month for Robert Lee Bennett Jr. A young man named Matthew "Red" Vernon told police that on the weekend of May 17 he was picked up by a white male driving a Lincoln Continental. The man gave him $20 for every pint of vodka he could drink. As they drove around, Vernon realized who had picked him up.

"I'll drink the next half pint if you give me the $20 now," Vernon told the man.

Bennett handed over the money.

With the $20 securely in his palm, Vernon opened the car door and jumped out, telling the driver, "I know you. You're Handcuff Man." Once on the sidewalk, Vernon stuck fingers down his throat and vomited up the vodka.

In the meantime, Jordan had recovered just enough for a productive interview with police investigators. He could not remember how he had been assaulted but he did recall Bennett being the last person he had been with before losing consciousness. He had no trouble picking his picture out of a group of photographs the police displayed.

Then Max Shrader picked out Bennett's picture as that of the man who had offered him money to drink five years before. "The reason I didn't forget it, is that I thought about it every day," the wounded man said.

It was after this second identification that *The Atlanta Journal Constitution* made the difficult decision to name Bennett as the suspect in the vicious Handcuff Man assaults.

A Plea Deal

After he was publicly fingered, Bennett issued vociferous

denials. "I am not the Handcuff Man!" he emphatically told reporters. He alleged that an Atlanta detective led hustlers to mistakenly identify him. "I think that [the detective] wants desperately to put this Handcuff Man behind bars," Bennett said. "And he thinks I'm that person. It doesn't happen to be true." Guy Notte, Bennett's attorney in the Atlanta cases, said his client was the victim of a "case of mistaken identity."

Free on $300,000 bail, Bennett resided, as he had in the past, with his disabled mother Annabelle Bennett.

In September 1991, Notte suggested an alternative culprit in the Florida attack on unemployed carpenter Gary Clapp. "Witchcraft is definitely involved in this," Notte asserted. The lawyer went on to say that close to Clapp's burning body there had been "decapitated chickens, decapitated goats, which smacks of the cult Santeria."

Santeria is the Afro-Cuban religion that combines elements of Roman Catholicism with aspects of the West African religion of Yoruba. The synthesized religion, which has many adherents in Florida, is controversial because animal sacrifice is one of its rituals.

In the Atlanta cases, Notte requested a change of venue because he claimed that "the tenor and intensity of publicity surrounding this case has severely prejudiced potential jurors." Fulton County prosecutor Dee Downs opposed the motion.

In June 1991, a tense and haggard-looking Bennett appeared in an Atlanta courtroom to waive extradition to Florida. He also complained bitterly about his conditions of incarceration. He said he was given no breakfast and had to go five hours without a blanket, pillow, or cigarettes. He elaborated that other prisoners were threatening him. "One … said he'd cut me," Bennett claimed.

Speaking on his client's behalf, Notte requested that Bennett be separated from his fellow prisoners. "We're not asking for special favors," Notte said. "We just want to ensure his safety. He's under a tremendous amount of pressure at the jail. He's under constant harassment."

When Gary Clapp learned that his attacker was on his way

to a trial in Florida, he was living in a tiny, government-sub-sidized apartment. His trousers pinned up around his thighs, holding and petting a black cat purring on his lap, he gave an interview to a *St. Petersburg Times* reporter. The amputee used a wheelchair to get around and talked about the possibility of being fitted with prosthetic legs. He fantasized about what he wished could happen to Bennett: "Truthfully, I'd like to see the same thing happen to him that happened to me." He also said that he wanted to be in the court when Bennett was tried although he knew it would be emotionally wrenching to have to face the man who had burned off most of his legs. "It can't be any harder than it's already been," Clapp said.

Before trial in Tampa, Clapp gave a deposition at the district attorney's office. Also present was Bennett, his lawyer Notte, the prosecutor, and a court reporter. One of Clapp's leg stumps began to bleed. Notte asked if Clapp was OK and if he wanted to delay the deposition. This solicitounesss angered Bennett. Much later, Notte told this writer that Bennett was "the coldest, most remorseless client I ever worked with."

Bennett had at first been determined to fight the charges. He spent $500,000 preparing his defense but lost his nerve at the last moment. He knew there would be a parade of men to testify that he had committed similar outrages against them. He also knew that the Tampa fire department had a videotape of Clapp burning. It all added up to enough evidence to get him a life sentence. As his attorney, Guy Notte, said, "In Florida, life means life. We just could not take the chance."

Prosecutors in both Tampa and Atlanta negotiated with Bennett's lawyers for a deal. They hammered out an agreement whereby Bennett would plead guilty to the attempted murder of Gary Clapp and two counts of aggravated assault in Atlanta, and could serve a 17-year sentence in Florida to run concurrently, rather than consecutively, with his sentence for the Atlanta crimes. The result of the deal, as Georgia's Fulton Country District Attorney Lewis Slaton acknowledged, would be that "he would serve no additional time for the Atlanta crimes."

Many gay activists were outraged by what they considered a lenient deal for a man who had terrorized their community for decades. "Good citizens need to step forward," urged Larry Pellegrini, president of the Lesbian and Gay Rights Chapter of the American Civil Liberties Union. "This is horrendous."

Lynn Cothren, co-chair of Queer Nation, said, "It's a sad situation when people can get away with torture, intimidation, and hate. There's obviously a problem with the system."

The Atlanta president of Parents and Friends of Lesbians and Gays (PFLAG), Judy Colbs, remarked, "Setting people on fire is setting people on fire, and it should not matter what the sexual orientation is. It goes back to prejudice. It affects and invades all parts of society."

Jeff Graham, a member of ACT-UP, an AIDS activist organization, also decried the plea bargain. "I think clearly if it were a case involving heterosexuals, that if he had done this to a woman [or] a straight man, that his sentence would be much greater than what it is," Graham speculated. "It has taken the Atlanta Police Department dozens of years to seriously investigate and solve this case. I think that clearly you've got a prejudiced judicial system in Atlanta, in Fulton County. I'm happy Tampa was able to put together the case."

The Atlanta Journal Constitution also denounced the plea agreement in an editorial entitled "Reject 'Handcuff case' deal."

The outrage of those quoted above was shared by at least one of Bennett's victims. Max Shrader, who Bennett burned in 1985, said prosecutors never contacted him to discuss the proposed plea bargain. "The judge had got to decide if the time fits the crime," Shrader observed. "I'm going to be there to tell him it does not."

Despite objections, the deal went through. On February 24, 1992, Bennett appeared in an Atlanta courtroom and pled guilty to two counts of aggravated assault. The sentence was 17 years in prison to run concurrently with the 17-year sentence that he was to serve in Florida for the attempted murder of Gary Clapp. The 44-year-old lawyer was also ordered to pay $65,000 in restitution for the medical bills of the two Atlanta victims, was banned for life from ever being in Fulton Country, and was ordered to see a psychiatrist.

"Did you pick up these two fellows?" Fulton Superior Court Judge Isaac Jenrette asked the defendant.

Bennett paused, then talked to his attorney.

"Did you pick up these two fellows?" Jenrette repeated.

"I'm pleading guilty to the two charges," Bennett said.

At the time of the sentencing, Bennett was free on $300,000 bond, under the conditions that he was not to leave the home he shared with his mother except on approved business, such as seeing his lawyers. He was to report on March 9, 1992, to start serving his sentence.

Bennett broke his agreement. He was spotted cruising the same Tampa street where he had picked up Gary Clapp. Tampa detective Bob Holland testified that he saw Bennett's car and followed it only to see the convicted torturer "talking with some guy leaning in his car window … What was weird was it was about the same time of the day [that] he met Gary Clapp there. It was almost a year to [the] date."

Because of this offense, Bennett was sent to jail two weeks earlier than scheduled.

The notorious Handcuff Man was initially put into solitary confinement, partly because he feared other prisoners. Tom Patterson, a supervisor at the North Florida Reception Center where Bennett was initially kept, described him as "an average inmate" and said "he hasn't cause any problems." Bennett was later moved to Liberty Correctional Institution, a "close custody" institution in west Florida.

Why?

What was behind the crimes of Robert Lee Bennett Jr.? Because he was frequently described as a "gay basher," his attacks were assumed to be the result of a homophobic homosexual's hatred for his own preferences directed outward.

For several years, Bennett denied he was gay. "However, he eventually admitted to being gay," Notte said. Was he, as most people supposed, a homophobic homosexual? Notte was unable to answer with certainty. "He never expressed any ho-mophobic sentiments to me," the attorney related to this writ-er.

However, the gay basher label is incomplete. As far as is known, Bennett never sought out homosexual men per se but men he believed were selling homosexual sexual services. Similar crimes are committed in the heterosexual community: Ted Bundy murdered young women; Joel Rifkin murdered women who were prostitutes.

Of course, there are strategic reasons why someone bent on robbery, rape, or other violence might target prostitutes of either sex. They are easy prey, being approachable and accus-tomed to odd requests. Being paid to drink alcohol does not set off an alarm in someone who may, as one hustler recalled, have been paid to urinate into a jar by a fetishist. Since prosti-tution is illegal, its perpetrators are less likely to report crimes against themselves to the authorities. All of these may have been factors in the Handcuff's Man choice of targets.

One of the victims, Michael Jordan, commented, "I feel sorry for this guy. I don't feel sorry for him in some ways but I feel sorry for him because I don't understand why he would do something like this. It's got to be something that [is] hurting him inside so bad or something."

Bennett was not insane. The office of his attorney, Guy Notte, had a team of psychiatrists in Florida examine him. "He was completely sane," Notte recalled. "He knew right from wrong. He had a behavioral disorder. That's an understate-ment."

He is known to have suffered from impotence, which may have been a factor in his burning the genitals of gay male pros-titutes. "If you can do something I want to do and can't," Notte speculated, "I might want to destroy your ability to do it."

While the Handcuff Man's sexual dysfunction may ex-plain his choice of victims, it does not explain his barbaric cruelty. After all, there are millions of men who suffer from impotence, and very few of them become violent.

Could sexual sadism have been behind his crimes? There

is no evidence that Bennett reached an orgasm while he was torturing his victims. Still, it cannot be ruled out, since his victims were usually unconscious. It is possible that, like a minority of other sex offenders who are described as generally impotent in non-violent situations, Bennett could only get erections or climaxes through criminal acts.

Contempt for those who sell sexual services is common in our culture. After all, prostitution is a criminal offense and "whore" a common term of derision. That common feeling may become exaggerated and obsessive for some people and Bennett could have been among them.

He is not known to have expressed remorse for his crimes of any concern for the damage done to his victims. Gary Clapp, who saw Bennett in the Tampa courtroom during his plea, said, "I don't think he'll ever feel sorry for anything he's done. This guy's a sick puppy."

Notte described Bennett as "very cold and clinical. He never would in so many words admit doing these things although he pled guilty."

Once during his imprisonment, in 1997, Bennett got a disciplinary write-up for disorderly conduct. Other than that, he appears to have been inoffensive as a prisoner. He did, however, break with Notte. Bennett attempted to bring an "ineffective assistance of counsel" claim against the lawyer because, according to Notte, "he believed that we had told him he would get out in two or three years." No attorney would take Bennett's case but he did find a lawyer who filed a suit against Notte to get Bennett's fee back.

That lawsuit was still pending when Bennett died of a stroke on April Fool's Day 1998. He took the reasons for his hatred of gay male prostitutes, and the genesis of his extraordinary cruelty, with him to his grave.

Bibliography

I give special thanks to Eric Freeley of the Fulton County District Attorney's Office for his assistance in preparing this article.

The case file of the Fulton County District Attorney's Office.

Carlton, Sue. *St. Petersburg Times.* "'Handcuff Man' leaves tragedy in his wake." October 20, 1991.

Greer, Richard. *The Atlanta Journal Constitution.* "Police want to question lawyer in attack." May 31, 1991.

Scruggs, Kathy. *The Atlanta Journal Constitution.* "Another victim IDs lawyer from photo lineup." June 2, 1991.

Greer, Richard. *The Atlanta Journal Constitution.* "Tampa burning victim surprised over charge." June 6, 1991.

Scruggs, Kathy. *The Atlanta Journal Constitution.* "Fear in the shadows." June 10, 1991.

Greer, Richard; Scruggs, Kathy. *The Atlanta Journal Constitution.* "He now faces charges here in two assaults." June 22, 1991.

Greer, Richard. *The Atlanta Journal Constitution.* "Homosexuals: Police drag feet when they don't like the victim.' August 5, 1991.

Greer, Richard. *The Atlanta Journal Constitution.* "Lawyer implicates Santeria in attack." September 5, 1991.

Greer, Richard. *The Atlanta Journal Constitution.* "Bennett linked to other incidents here." October 9, 1991.

Greer, Richard. *The Atlanta Journal Constitution.* "Guilty plea in 'Handcuff' case." Febrary 14, 1992.

Greer, Richard. *The Atlanta Journal Constitution.* "Good citizens need to step forward." February 15, 1992.

Greer, Richard. *The Atlanta Journal Constitution*. "Family ties aided 'Handcuff' suspect." February 24, 1992.

Greer, Richard. *The Atlanta Journal Constitution*. "'Handcuff Man' Gets 17 years in prison." February 24, 1992.

Scruggs, Kathy. *The Atlanta Journal Constitution*. "Police insensitive, activists say." March 1, 1992.

The Atlanta Journal Constitution. "Bennett begins 17-year sentence in Florida." March 9, 1992.

Kaplan, Paul. *The Atlanta Journal Constitution*. "News Update." April 26, 1992.

Greer, Richard. *FineLine: The Newsletter On Journalism Ethics*. "Newspaper nabs Atlanta's Dahmer." September 1991.

CHAPTER 7

The Baffling Brutality of the Briley Brothers: Bad Seeds or Fearsome Family Secrets?

Discussions of the root causes of criminality often focus on the relative weight of biological and environmental factors in creating a dangerous personality. The Nature vs. Nurture controversy asks: are psychopaths born or made?

In many cases, poor nurturing was clearly a cause of catastrophe. With staggering regularity, dangerous criminals have family backgrounds of neglect and gaspingly hideous abuse.

However, there are also instances in which violent individuals were raised in what appear to have been stable and loving families. Cases in which siblings raised apart became similarly criminal suggest the possibility of problems rooted in genetics as do instances in which violent psychopaths raised in (apparently) loving adoptive homes were found to have had criminal birthmothers or biological fathers.

The classic 1956 film, *The Bad Seed*, was based on the "Nature" argument. In that motion picture, Rhoda Penmark (Patty McCormack) is the much-loved child of Christine Penmark (Nancy Kelly) and Col. Kenneth Penmark (William Hopper). Little Rhoda has been raised in affluence with parents who lavish love on her. The child is revealed to be a murderous psychopath. The apparent reason is that she inherited a defective, homicidal brain from her grandmother who was an infamous serial murderer.

The baffling story of the Briley brothers begs for further study that might illuminate the causes of their bizarre and brutal criminal careers. Their history seems to defy both sides of the Nature Vs. Nurture debate—and calls for further investigation into the backgrounds, both biological and environmental, of this astonishing trio of terrifying psychopaths.

Boys Who Liked Dangerous Pets

Linwood, James, and Anthony Briley were born and raised in a financially secure husband and wife home. The parents appeared to be emotionally stable. There is no information suggesting they were abused physically, sexually, or emotionally. African-Americans, they grew up in a racially integrated middle-class Richmond, Virginia neighborhood. Neighbors thought of the Briley brothers as friendly boys who helped neighbors fix cars or mow lawns.

However, it is known that, from early childhood, the brothers had a chilling hobby: they liked to collect dangerous pets like piranhas and boa constrictors. They relished feeding live mice to a boa constrictor.

Their father, James Briley, Sr., became so anxious because of his sons' behaviors that he padlocked his bedroom door when he slept.

At this point, it might be well to pause and consider what the above suggests. Despite the sadistic tendencies his sons' demonstrated, and despite his own fear of them, there is no evidence Dad Briley sought therapeutic intervention. Was this because he was indifferent to their mental health? Was it because he had done things in raising them that he did not want outsiders to know about? The answers to these questions are unknown.

A 16-Year-Old Commits a Senseless Murder

It is known that Linwood was only 16 when he committed his first murder—a crime distinguished by its senselessness. He shot a rifle from his bedroom window at next-door neighbor Orline Christian, 57, as she hung laundry in her backyard.

This homicide almost escaped detection. People thought Christian, grieving because her husband had recently died, had suffered a heart attack. However, as *Times-Dispatch* reporters Reed Williams and Bill McKelway write, "When the funeral home returned the robe she had been wearing, the family noticed a small, bloody hole in the back." The corpse was re-examined and the bullet hole discovered.

After police were notified, a detective stood at the window in Christian's home and determined that the bullet could only have been shot from the Briley residence. The weapon was found there.

"I heard she had heart problems," Linwood callously commented when he confessed. "She would have died soon anyway." Because of Linwood's age, this murder led to him serving only one year in a juvenile detention facility. James soon was sentenced to a similar facility for firing on a cop during a pursuit.

As is too often the case, time in juvenile detention facilities failed to curb the anti-social tendencies of Linwood and James and in 1979, the two of them, together with brother Anthony and friend Duncan Meekins, commenced a crime spree that terrified Richmond and surrounding areas. Sheriff C. T. Woody observed, "Linwood was the leader." Victims of the Briley attacks included blacks and whites, men and women, young and old, poor and affluent.

Cruel Crime Spree

On March 12, 1979, shortly before 9:00 p.m., Linwood knocked on the door of William and Virginia Bucher. He claimed he had car trouble and needed to use their phone to call AAA. Williams and McKelway report, "Bucher said he would be glad to call for him and told the man to give him his AAA card. [Linwood] fumbled around and pulled out a card. Just when Bucher cracked open the screen door to accept the card, the stranger produced a gun and barged inside." The other three rushed inside. The gang tied up the couple and looted their house. Then they doused rooms with gasoline and even put some on William Bucher's leg. As they left, they tossed a lit match.

Incredibly, the panicked William was able to free both himself and his wife from their restraints. The couple escaped the inferno. The Buchers are the only known survivors of a Briley attack.

The Briley gang invaded the home of Michael McDuffie on March 21, shot him dead, and looted his house.

On April 9, they followed Mary Gowen, 76, to her home. They raped, robbed, and shot her dead just outside her house.

On the Fourth of July, the gang saw Christopher Philips, 17, hanging around Linwood's parked car. Thinking Philips intended to break into the vehicle, they dragged him to a near-by backyard. Linwood crushed Philips' head with a cinder-block.

Country-and-western disc jockey and musician, John "Johnny G." Gallagher was performing with his band at the Log Cabin dancehall on September 14. Gallagher stepped out-side during a break, Linwood forced Gallagher into the trunk of his own car. The gang drove to an abandoned mill, removed Gallagher from the trunk, shot him dead, and threw him into the James River. Then they divided up the haul from his wal-let: $6.

Fishermen found Gallagher's body on September 16.

On September 30, the gang followed Mary Wilfong home to her apartment. They surrounded her outside the door. Lin-wood crushed her head with a baseball bat. The group invad-ed her home and robbed goods from the house.

The group invaded the home of blind Blanche Page and her boarder Charles Garner on October 5. Williams and McK-elway write that Linwood "bashed the head of 75-year-old Blanche Page as she lay in bed, splashing the ceiling with blood." They elaborate, "Garner's body was discovered with knives, scissors and a carving fork sticking out of it. The Briley gang lit a fire on his back with the Yellow Pages."

On the morning of October 19, James promised a judge

he would avoid trouble while on parole for 1973 malicious wounding and robbery convictions. That evening, James led the gang to the home of neighbor Harvey Wilkerson. Wilkerson lived with his five months pregnant wife, Judy Barton, 23, and five-year-old son Harvey.

Wilkerson saw the four and closed and locked his front door. Seeing this fearful response, they went to his door and knocked. Murderpedia reports, "Terrified by their response if he refused them entry, Wilkerson allowed them in." Wilkerson and Barton were overpowered and bound with duct tape. Linwood forced Barton into the kitchen where he raped her. When Linwood finished, Meekins raped her. Murderpedia writes that after Meekins finished raping Barton, "Linwood dragged Barton back into the living room, briefly rummaged the premises for valuables and then left the house. The three remaining gang members covered their victims with sheets."

James told Meekins, "You've got to get one." Meekins shot Wilkerson dead. James did the same to Barton and little Harvey.

Cruising police heard shots and saw gang members racing away in a car. Within a few days, all four were taken into police custody.

A search of the home in which the Briley brothers lived showed the gang had kept a scrapbook of newspaper articles about their crimes.

Richmond Police Detective Leroy Morgan had been a close friend of victim John Gallagher so he was asked to help interrogate the Brileys. Morgan noticed a distinctive ring on Linwood's finger: a blue and white ring sporting a black sliver. Morgan recognized it as Gallagher's and became instantly nauseous.

Meekins avoided the death penalty and accepted a sentence of life that included the possibility of parole as part of a plea agreement in which he testified against the Brileys. Prosecutors Robert J. Rice and Warren Von Schuch also promised Meekins that they would speak for his release when he went before a parole board.

Virginia's "triggerman" rule means that a murderer who

did not do the actual killing is ineligible for the death penalty. Since it could not be proved that Anthony had committed any first-hand murder, he was sentenced to life imprisonment, also with parole eligibility, even though he had not cooperated with police.

Linwood was sentenced to death for John Gallagher's murder and James received death sentences in the murders of Judy Barton and son Harvey. A judge commented, "This was the vilest rampage of rape, murder, and robbery that the court has seen in thirty years." Linwood and James were taken to the Death Row at Mecklenburg Correctional Center.

On May 31, 1983, six inmates escaped from that Death Row. Linwood and James were the ringleaders of the escape that was the largest Death Row breakout in United States history.

Williams and McKelway report, "Six death-row inmates, including the two Brileys, escaped after overpowering guards and exiting the prison by staging a bomb hoax. In fact, the bomb was a television set carried on a stretcher and covered with a sheet. One of the escapees 'cooled' the device with blasts from a fire extinguisher."

The group took guards and a female nurse hostage. Lighter fluid was tossed on the guards but escaped murderer Willie Lloyd Turner prevented James from throwing a match. Another escaped murderer, Wilbert Evans, prevented Linwood from raping the nurse.

Two escapees were soon re-captured. Linwood and James parted company with the remaining two and took refuge in an uncle's Philadelphia home. They were on the lam for nineteen days.

On June 19, 1983, FBI and police captured Linwood and James. They returned to Death Row. Their uncle was arrested for harboring them.

Linwood was executed in Virginia's electric chair on October 12, 1984. Sheriff Woody said Linwood "was sweating, he was shaking" when escorted to the death chamber. James was electrocuted on April 18, 1985.

Anthony Briley has been repeatedly denied parole during

his imprisonment. Although prosecutors Robert J. Rice and Warren Von Schuch have spoken to parole boards on behalf of Duncan Meekins, he too has been denied parole. Von Schuch has asserted, "There could not be a graver injustice than to have Duncan Meekins serve the same amount of time as Anthony Briley."

Part of the reason for Meekins' continuing imprisonment may be the vocal opposition of victims' relatives to his release. Robert Jones, nephew of Harvey Wilkerson, reporters, "I have not healed, nor will I heal, nor will I forgive." Jones recalled that he usually stayed with Uncle Harvey during summers – and would probably have been killed in the rampage if he had not had tonsillitis in 1979.

Shurrane Webb, sister of Judy Barton, wrote to the parole board, saying, "Who's to say he won't get out of here and do it again?"

Because his cooperation branded him a "snitch" in the view of fellow inmates, Meekins has been imprisoned outside Virginia under an assumed name.

Meanness Most Mysterious

The Briley brothers present a puzzle to anyone wanting to understand the reasons for criminality. They were not the products of poverty or a broken home. However, it is obvious that something went terribly, terribly wrong with these three young men. Sheriff Woody stated, "I've never seen anybody meaner than the Brileys."

What was the source of that meanness? It is possible abuses went on behind closed doors. It is also possible that they simply did not receive the affection in their early years that is necessary to develop healthy personalities.

There is also the possibility that these three were born with defective brains. However, unlike the creepy child protagonist of *The Bad Seed*, it is not known that the Brileys had a peculiarly homicidal ancestor.

The reasons for the malformed personalities of the Brileys are currently mysterious. Intensive research into the biological heritage of this family and the manner in which these men were raised should be done in an attempt to learn what was behind the mysterious meanness of the Briley brothers. Such research may even unearth clues that could apply more generally to the frustrating questions that cluster around the interplay of Nature and Nurture in the creation of violent criminals.

Bibliography

"Linwood Earl Briley." Murderpedia.

"The Briley Brothers." http://www.youtube.com/watch?v=aa-xrxQ9iN8.

Williams, Reed. "Briley Brothers: More victims' kin say they oppose parole for Meekins." *Times-Dispatch*. June 27, 2009.

Williams, Reed; McKelway, Bill. "The Briley brothers terrorized the Richmond area." *Times-Dispatch*. http://www.vatalent.com/newsa.php?news_id=977.

Williams, Reed. "Briley gang member Duncan Meekins denied parole." *Times-Dispatch*. August 14, 2009.

Williams, Reed; McKelway, Bill. "Officials seek release for Briley brothers accomplice." *Times-Dispatch*. May 13, 2009.

Williams, Reed. "Relative of slaying victims opposes release of Briley brothers' accomplice." *Times-Dispatch*. June 17, 2009.

CHAPTER 8

How Violence Derailed the Life and Career of Barbara Payton

Barbara Payton was filming *Bride of the Gorilla*, a horror movie that became a camp classic, when she met actor Tom Neal in July 1951. Barbara was engaged to star Franchot Tone who was in New York. Despite this, she romanced Tom.

Franchot returned to California in August. Tom had moved into the apartment in which Barbara lived. Barbara and Tom set their wedding date for September 14, 1951.

On the morning of September 13, Barbara borrowed Tom's car, saying she needed it for a "business appointment." She drove to Franchot and the romantic pair enjoyed time together. Franchot and Barbara walked into her apartment at 1:30 a.m. Tom and Franchot quarreled. Barbara urged Franchot, "Get rid of Tom."

"Let's settle this thing outside!" Franchot challenged.

John O'Dowd writes in Kiss Tomorrow Goodbye: The Barbara Payton Story, "The threesome had moved to the front patio of Barbara's apartment when an adrenaline-powered Tom delivered a punch that literally sent his opponent airborne, knocking him a distance of twelve feet before slamming him into the ground … Tom then pounced on Franchot, battering him in a brutal and bone-crunching assault." Barbara intervened. Tom slugged her in the eye.

A bystander called police, Tom went to jail and an ambulance rushed Franchot to a hospital.

Brawl Grabs Headlines

TOM NEAL KNOCKS OUT TONE IN LOVE FIST FIGHT! and similar headlines eclipsed news of the Korean war.

On September 23, Franchot and Barbara together gave statements to the district attorney. Four days later, Franchot told that D.A. that he would not press charges against Tom.

Franchot and Barbara married on September 28, 1951.

The apex of this tumultuous triangle was born on November 26, 1927. In her early 20s, she decided on an acting career. Barbara Payton's big break came with her starring role in *Trapped* (1949) opposite Lloyd Bridges. Bridges played the leader of a counterfeiting gang and Barbara his girlfriend. O'Dowd notes, "Barbara seemed to infuse some of her real-life characteristics of wide-eyed innocence mixed with a kind of reckless self-assurance into the role."

The positive reviews for Barbara's performance in *Trapped* led to her being cast opposite Jimmy Cagney in Kiss Tomorrow Goodbye (1950). Her acting was widely praised. On the Internet Movie Database, one person describes her as "realistic" while another asserts that "beautiful" Barbara's "tension and wild lilting ferocity and fear" burns through the movie "like a fuse." Another calls her "resonant and convincing."

Franchot Tone announced their engagement in October 1950.

Barbara played in Drums in the Deep South (1951) with Guy Madison—with whom she also played off-screen. In mid-1951, Franchot barged into Barbara's apartment to find her making love with Guy.

"I'm engaged to this girl and I'm going to marry her!" Franchot shouted. "Are you?"

Guy answered, "No, I can't. I'm already married."

Thrilled to see two men squabbling over her, Barbara punched a pillow, kicked her legs in the air, and laughed. This quarrel might be seen as foreshadowing the fistfight that would follow it.

The Shower of Spit

Barbara and Franchot were in a nightclub on October 29, 1951 when Franchot spotted gossip columnist Florabel Muir who had lambasted Barbara and he in print. Franchot shambled to Muir and yelled. She said, "You talk as though you're mad at me."

"Yes, I am," he replied. "So mad, in fact, that I could just spit in your face. In fact, that's just what I'm going to do." The wad of spit caught her in the eye.

Cops carted Franchot to jail. He paid a $400 fine for battery on December 11, 1951.

While still married, Barbara re-kindled her romance with Tom. Tom accompanied Barbara on a promotional tour for *Bride of the Gorilla*. Tom was out of sight when Barbara hooked up with six drunken cowboys in town for a rodeo. She encouraged them to fight for her favors leading to arrests.

In March 1952, Franchot divorced Barbara.

Barbara traveled to Britain to make two low-budget films *Four-Sided Triangle* (1953) and *The Flanagan Boy* (1953) that was titled *Bad Blonde* in America. Both films tanked, getting negative reviews and a small audience.

Tom and Barbara split in November 1953.

Barbara returned to Hollywood. She co-starred with Sonny Tufts in the comedy Run for the Hills. Sonny plays an insurance actuary who fears nuclear war. Barbara is his wife. The couple moves into a cave. The film failed but Barbara's performance was good. O'Dowd writes that she "shows an endearingly flighty, almost Gracie Allen-like quality in her acting, revealing a natural flair in her comic delivery."

Barbara starred in *Murder is My Beat* (1954), playing suspected murderer Eden Lane. O'Dowd writes, "Barbara's wonderfully subtle performance" is "well-regarded today by a myriad of film critics." Critic Dennis Schwartz states that the movie's "slight narrative is enhanced by the edgy performance of Barbara Payton, who never tips her hand if she's guilty or innocent."

Although Barbara's performance was excellent, the film

was a financial flop—and the last motion picture in which she ever acted.

Barbara vacationed in Mexico, returning home in October 1955. On October 14, she was arrested because checks she had written were returned for insufficient funds. A friend paid $1,500 bail and she was released from jail.

Barbara pled guilty to issuing a worthless check on December 27, 1955. The judge agreed to suspend a jail sentence if she paid a $100 fine. A friend paid it.

Barbara spent much time traveling from America to Mexico and back again.

Tanned, slim, and looking gorgeous, Barbara held an August 12, 1958, press conference on to announce her comeback plans.

But filmmakers did not hire her.

She was hired as a hostess at a restaurant in 1959, sometimes seating celebrities at whose homes she had once dined. She was fired for coming to work drunk. She worked at a dry cleaner's in 1960 and was fired for the same reason. She worked at cocktail serving, hair shampooing, and gas pumping during the early 1960s. She turned to prostitution, charging $300. When a customer left her $100, she was upset. He said, "Three hundred was a long time ago. I don't want to hurt you, Barbara, but you've lost a little since then."

When Barbara was arrested for prostitution on February 7, 1962, her price had dropped to $40.

On July 21, 1962, Barbara called police to report that the hotel room she shared with diaper seller Robert Sherry had been broken into and that the invaders had beaten Barbara. Sherry backed up her story.

An officer drove Barbara and Sherry to the police station. By the time they got there, their story had changed. They said a teenaged gang had dragged her to a lot where they beat her and attempted to rape her. Both gave vague descriptions of the attackers. Officers promised to investigate and paid for a cab to drive the couple home.

The next morning a cop found Barbara, wearing only a

bathing suit and sweater, unconscious on a bench. He arrested her for public intoxication. She was soon released on $21 bail.

The following Saturday, July 28, 1962, police responded to a complaint of loud noise in an apartment in which a woman was "cavorting naked" before "an open window." The woman was Barbara. She was arrested for drunk and disorderly conduct. A friend bailed her out.

In March 1963, a customer stabbed Barbara. She required 38 stitches from her stomach to her thighs. She later stated, "Some filthy drunk got mad at me when I wouldn't do what he wanted."

Her price had slid to $5 for quick fellatio in parked cars.

On October 17, 1963, Barbara stood before Judge Bernard S. Seiber convicted of prostitution. Seiber admonished, "I find it wholly regrettable that a person of the obvious talents and capabilities of you, Miss Payton, has sunk to such low depths. I do hope, however, that there is still a germ of respectability somewhere within you that will enable you to be rehabilitated." She paid a $150 fine.

The stabbing led publisher Holloway House to become interested in Barbara's story. They enlisted columnist Leo Guild to ghostwrite it. She agreed to talk into a tape recorder so he could put the book together from the recordings.

Published in 1963, Guild titled it *I Am Not Ashamed* after something Barbara had supposedly said. There were reports that she was paid $1,000 or $2,000 or that she was paid not with money but with wine! The book was a poor seller.

Awhile after the book was published, Barbara was hired as a motel housekeeper. She lost the job due to drunkenness.

On April 1, 1967, Tom Neal walked into a restaurant and informed the owners, who were close friends of his, that he had just shot and killed his wife Gail. His buddies laughed, thinking it was an April Fool's joke.

But Tom, who had almost beaten Franchot to death, had really killed this time. Tom said he had accused Gail of infidelity and that had "grabbed a pistol from the coffee table and began waving it around." He said it discharged accidentally when he tried to take it from her. He was charged with murder because the shot went through the back of her head. There are reports that Barbara was in the court on Tom's November 1965 sentencing hearing.

Convicted of manslaughter, he was sentenced to one to fifteen years in prison. Barbara wrote him during the early years he was incarcerated.

In February 1967, two sanitation workers saw what they thought was a large bag of trash beside a dumpster. When they got closer, they saw it was a woman. Despite chilly air, she wore only a shift and flip-flops. Dried blood was caked around her mouth and nose and her limbs were covered with bruises. Her hair had two inches of dark roots below the blond hair that was bunched into a disorderly bun.

To the men's shock, she breathed! They rushed for help. Newspapers were soon filled with the story that the derelict was Barbara Payton who had been living on the streets for over a month.

Doctors determined that she had passed out from drinking. She was taken to the Los Angeles County General Hospital charity ward. She was diagnosed with "chronic alcoholism."

After a brief hospital stay, she was driven to her parents' home. She died on May 8, 1967.

In her later years, Barbara wrote poetry. Some was published in journals but only one brief poem is known. It is a haunting reminder of the star who crashed.

Love is a memory.
Time cannot kill
The cherished tune,
gay and absurd,
And the music unheard.

Bibliography

Barbara Payton biography. Internet Movie Database. http://

www.imdb.com/name/nm0668510/bio

"Kiss Tomorrow Goodbye." Internet Movie Database user reviews. http://www.imdb.com/title/tt0042648/reviews

O'Dowd, John. *Kiss Tomorrow Goodbye: The Barbara Payton Story.* BearManor Media. 2006.

Payton, Barbara. *I Am Not Ashamed.* Holloway House. 1963.

Schwartz, Dennis. Ozus' World Movie Reviews. Murder is My Beat. "Packs some punch." http://homepages.sover.net/~ozus/murderismybeat.htm

CHAPTER 9

"Children of God," Pedophilia and a "Little Prince" Named Davidito

In the late 1960s, minister David Berg, evangelized hippies and surfers in Huntington Beach, California. The middle-aged preacher, born in 1919, found young people receptive to his unusual message blending fundamentalist Christianity with liberal sexual ethics. As Berg's followers grew, Berg dubbed them the "Children of God" in 1968. The name was changed to "Family of Love" in 1978 and later to its present "Family International," often called "The Family" or TF. It has adherents in many countries, often living in communes that were originally called "colonies" but are now called "homes."

Berg taught that Christians must follow the Bible but asserted he was the Christian prophet for this era. "Mo Letters" informed his followers of new divine revelations. When he died in 1994, his widow, Karen Zerby, succeeded him as leader.

Converts were encouraged to take new, Biblical names. Berg was often called "Moses David" or "Dad" and later "Grandpa." Zerby is often called "Mama" or "Mama Maria."

In classic counter-culture language, Berg declared himself against "the System" which he believed hypocritically distorted God's Word into a sexually repressive message. In Mo Letters, he denounced "System" teachings against masturbation, writing, "Enjoy yourself and sex and what God has given you to enjoy, without fear or condemnation! For 'perfect love casts out all fear,' for "fear hath torment,' particularly sexual fears [which] can be physical torture!" He did not want his followers to suffer as he did "the horrors of such sexual frustrations and condemnations."

Berg encouraged female followers to abandon bras and even publicly expose their breasts. His 1970 poem "Mountin' Maid!" declared, "I am for the mini-blouse/Or the see-through at my house ... Let those mountains be more visible/And their clothing more divisible."

However, he taught that male homosexuality was sinful, a teaching that continues today among the organization which excommunicates men for same-sex acts. Women were taught to avoid exclusive lesbianism but permitted bisexuality.

TF came under renewed scrutiny in 2005 when Berg's stepson Ricky Rodriguez murdered a member and then killed himself.

Flirty Fishing Flashes and Fizzles

In 1974, Berg introduced a controversial conversion method called "Flirty Fishing" or "FFing." Writer Stephen A. Kent observed that Berg advocated, "COG members practice recruitment and resource acquisition through sexual activities."

Berg urged females to become "hookers for Jesus."

James T. Richardson reports, "'Flirty fishing' involved witnessing to outsiders in such a way that it might even involve sex between female members" and potential converts. Richardson notes, "The women had to be willing (as did their husbands [if married]) for them to 'go all the way' if it was deemed necessary in order to 'reach someone for Christ.'"

The practice outraged traditional Christians who believed the Bible forbids non-marital sex. Some people left the organization because of FFing. Babies born as a result of sexual proselytizing were called "Jesus Babies" in the organization.

Missions in Europe sometimes opened discotheques as a creative way to proselytize. A disco in Italy was raided in 1979 and some members were charged with prostitution.

Flirty Fishing was officially ended in 1988 with anyone

continuing to practice it subject to excommunication.

In 1991, three years after FFing was dropped the Italian prostitution case finally went to trial. Judges ruled the activities were not legally prostitution as the money gathered was considered "a personal contribution to the humanitarian aims that the sect always claimed to pursue." Charges were dismissed.

Pedophilia and the Little Prince Called Davidito

Some of Berg's most alarming teachings appeared to condone pedophilia and incest. Mo Letters from the 1970s discuss a babysitter who masturbated and fellated Berg when he was only three years old. Berg asserted her actions did not do him "any harm."

In 1973, he wrote, "Incest, or certain forms of sex with certain specified close relatives was not made illegal until the Mosaic Law 2600 years after Creation." He also wrote, "Marriages of brothers and sisters, mothers and sons and even fathers and daughters were very common in ancient times and were not even considered incestuous, much less illegal."

Karen Zerby gave birth to a "Jesus Baby" in 1975. The product of FFing and stepson of David Berg was named David Moses Zerby. Later, his name was legally changed to Richard Peter Smith and still later to Richard Rodriguez. As a child, he was nicknamed "Davidito."

Berg and Zerby believed Rick was a "divine prince," destined to take over the ministry. Raised without hypocritical "System" sexual inhibitions, he would grow into a mighty religious leader.

In 1982, the Family International published a book entitled The Story of Davidito. It purports to be the story of his early childhood as told by one of his nannies. That nanny, Sara, writes that she hopes the rearing of Davidito will begin a "Childcare Revolution" and exclaims, "Thank You Jesus! A new example was set before us."

She writes that she and other nannies fellated Davidito to "clean" his penis. He was also allowed to watch adults having sex. Sara writes that readers learning about "Davidito's sexy experiences" should "prayerfully" learn from them and "follow the Lord's leadings." The book is heavily illustrated with photographs, some of which show the boy and an adult woman cuddling, both naked.

In a Mo Letter, Berg proclaimed, "You can throw a lot of that old stuff out! We're writing a whole new childcare series called The Davidito Series ... Davidito was to become an example to the world and inspire lots of childcare material! Thank God!"

The book was cited in a child custody case in the United Kingdom. Justice Ward stated, "I am totally satisfied that there was widespread sexual abuse of young children and teenagers by adult members of The Family, and that this abuse occurred to a significantly greater extent within The Family than occurred in society outside it." Referring to the Mo Letter quoted above, Justice Ward commented, "Berg was, in my judgment, quite clear [in] giving his approval to whatever was being written and he was assuming responsibility for it. It is naïve of The Family to seek to distance the leadership from this book and cast the sole blame upon Sara."

However, the court allowed the mother to keep physical custody of the child but after receiving assurances she would not allow what the judge called "sexual shenanigans." The court retained legal custody.

The Family Shores Up Its Image

Berg issued a statement in 1988 declaring, "We do not approve of sex with minors and hereby renounce any writings of anyone in the Family which may seem to do so! We absolutely forbid it!"

Referring to the Davidito book without specifically naming it, Berg called it only "the writer's account of her own personal experience and opinions."

In 1993, French police raided two TF communities because of sex abuse allegations. However, the children were soon returned to their parents and no charges brought.

The Family called a press conference in Britain to assert that it has changed. "House Shepherd" Gideon Scott said, "We are trying to show that we are normal people who believe sincerely in our religion and love our children. We do not promote or encourage sexual activity between adults and minors. Sexual relationships are not allowed in our communities between adults and those under 21."

Questioned about Berg's writings regarding children and sex, Scott called them "theological speculation."

The organization's 2003 Charter Amendments states, "Anyone 18 years or older who does anything sexual whatsoever with anyone under the age of 14 will be excommunicated."

Rick commits murder and then suicide

Rick, formerly "Davidito," was in his late teens when he started deriding the Family's beliefs and practices. He broke with the group in 2001. He and his fiancée Elixcia Garcia issued a statement that "we cannot continue to condone or be party to what we feel is an abusive manipulative organization that teaches false doctrine."

The couple married but Rick could not forget the abuses he had suffered in the name of a "sexually free" childcare revolution. He was often depressed.

He was 30 when he invited Family member Angela Smith to his Tucson, Arizona apartment on January 8, 2005. She was reported to have acted as his nanny—and engaged in sexual acts with him when he was a child. He stabbed her to death.

Then Rick drove to Blythe, California. There he made videotape in which he ranted about his childhood miseries. He bitterly denounced the "perverts" in the "cult." At one point he said, "My own mother! ... How can you do that to kids? How can you do that to kids and sleep at night?" He asserted that "thousands of Family kids" had "been abused." He bitterly asked, "Where's our apology?" and then answered, "They're not even fuckin' sorry." At the end of the videotape he predicts that the people who abused him are "going down.

So with that happy thought, I shall leave you."

After making the tape, he went to his car and drove around. Finally, he parked his car and ended his life with a shot in the head. Police found his body in the vehicle early on the morning of January 9, 2005.

On January 18, 2005, The Family issued a statement about the tragedy. It commented, "Our prayers are that Ricky's actions and the pursuant attention from the media won't whip up a new reaction at the behest of our detractors, which will once again cause harm, trauma and abuse to the innocent." That statement reiterated that the organization has a "zero tolerance policy regarding sexual interaction between adults and underage minors."

Bibliography

Bennett, Will. "Cult denies child sex abuse." The Independent. 1993-07-02. http://www.xfamily.org/index.php/The_Independent:_Cult_denies_child_sex_abuse

Borowik, Claire. "'International Christian Fellowship' Issues Statement." January 18, 2005. http://www.newdaynews.com/resource/davidito/borowick-01.htm

"Child Abuse?! – An Official Statement from the Founders of the Children of God!" http://www.xfamily.org/index.php/Child_Abuse%3F!

Charter Amendments 2003. http://www.xfamily.org/images/c/c5/CharterAmendments.pdf

Kent, Stephen A. "Lustful Prophet: A Psychosexual Historical Study of the Children of God's Leader, David Berg." 2000. Department of Sociology, University of Alberta.

Richardson, James T. "Update on 'The Family': Organizational Change and Development in a Controversial New Religious

Group." University of Nevada. http://www.thefamilyinterna-tional.org/dossier/books/book1/chapter2.htm

"Ricky Rodriguez Video Transcript." http://www.xfamily.org/index.php/Ricky_Rodriguez_Video_Transcript

"Story of Davidito." From XFamily – Children of God. http://www.xfamily.org/index.php/Story_of_Davidito

"The Children of God and The Family in Italy." Center for Studies on New Religions. http://www.cesnur.org/testi/The-Family/italy.htm

"The Davidito Book: Findings of the High Court of Justice Family Division, U.K." http://www.exfamily.org/the-family/court/davidito-book.htm

Wright, Stuart A. "From 'Children of God' to 'The Family': Movement Adaptation and Survival." Lamar University. http://www.thefamilyinternational.org/dossier/books/book1/chapter8.htm

CHAPTER 10

The Brutal Burning of David Rothenberg

On the evening of March 3, 1983, six-year-old David Rothenberg slept peacefully in a California motel room. David's father, Charles Rothenberg, 42, was divorced from David's mother, Marie Rothenberg, but frequently took the boy on trips.

A few days before, he had picked the boy up from his New York home to take him on what Charles said would be a week-long trip. As David slept, Charles poured kerosene around the room, lit a match, ran from the room, and sped away in a white car. Later Charles claimed he intended to stay in that room because he wanted David and he to die together but panicked. Seeing the fire, someone called police. By the time the ambulance arrived at the motel, Charles had driven back to its parking lot. Charles watched emergency personnel carry David into the ambulance.

Charles followed the ambulance to the University of California Irvine Medical Center. Doctors in the burn unit did not expect David, who had severe burns over 90% of his body, to survive.

In the lobby, Charles wired this message to Marie: "By the time you get this telegram, I will have terminated my existence. David has been in a very bad accident." Western Union gave Marie this ominous message on March 4, 1983.

Police called Marie's boss and told him David had been

badly injured in a fire. The boss informed Marie that David was hospitalized in California. Marie flew to California. She was horrified when she saw David, recalling, "He was bandaged from head to toe and smeared all over with creams. His eyes were so badly burned they popped out of his head. His fingers were black and bloody and his lips were gone."

Doctors were pleasantly surprised when it became evident David would survive. However, survival would necessitate terrible continuing pain. Marie wrote in an article published in People, "To take the burned tissue off, the doctors put David in a whirlpool containing a bleach solution and brushed off the bad skin. In the beginning they used pigskin and cadaver skin to cover him temporarily by stapling it to him. When he was surgically ready for real skin, the doctors took the top layer of skin from part of his body not burned and laid it on him in mesh graphs. Later that would grow together."

As physicians treated David, Charles was the target of a nationwide manhunt. Police arrested Charles, who was wearing a pin stating "Kids Are Special," in San Francisco on March 9, 1983.

Charles confessed trying to kill David. Charles said Marie threatened to prevent Charles from seeing David again when she discovered Charles had taken him to California. Marie says she was angered to learn where they were but does not recall making that threat although she admits that she might have. Charles told police, "If I couldn't have him, nobody could."

Convicted of attempted murder and assault with a deadly weapon, Charles was sentenced to 13 years imprisonment.

Although the relationship between Charles and Marie had been troubled, no one could have predicted it would reach its nadir in this hideous atrocity.

Marie recalled being drawn to Charles because, like her, he lacked a happy family background. She remembered, "I thought we'd both work hard to build what we had never had in our early years."

A child of divorce, Marie spent her childhood shuttling between an abusive mother and an abusive stepmother. Marie quit high school and went to work in a factory so she could live on her own.

Product of Orphanages

Charles was born to a single mother. He spent his childhood shuffling between Mom and orphanages. As a young adult, he usually worked as a waiter. He also racked up a lengthy arrest record for thefts and bad checks.

In a manuscript about his life, Charles described his feelings when David was born: "What a joy! God, I was so happy!"

However, he also said that when he touched the baby, "David was like paper." Psychologist Andrew Savicky observed that this statement indicates Charles perceived his son as "thing." Charles also said, "Children are the greatest commodity we have in life," reinforcing the probability that Charles could not see David as a person.

Marie recalled, "Charles was a proud, possessive, and overindulgent father ... He regularly took David shopping and bought him 50 or 60 dollars' worth of toys, until our apartment was cluttered with enough games, puzzles, and toys to stock a store."

Once when David cried, Charles blamed Marie and beat her. This and similar incidents led Marie to divorce Charles in 1978. Charles continued to visit David regularly.

In early 1983, Charles was fired from a restaurant for suspected stealing. The business was later vandalized and a warrant was issued for his arrest. That probably motivated him to want to leave New York.

In late February 1983, Charles told Marie he was taking David for a week's vacation in the Catskills. Instead, Charles took David to California, planning to visit Knott's Berry Farm and Disneyland. Rain prevented those visits so Charles called Marie and requested more time with David. Charles let it slip that they were in California that may have led Marie to threaten to block Charles from visiting David when she got him back.

The Daddy Who Damaged

While David was still hospitalized, he asked Marie, "Mommy, did my daddy do this to me?"

Marie sadly replied that he had.

David then asked, "Why did Daddy do this to me?" Marie said Charles was "sick" and "went crazy." David burst into helpless sobs. He later delared, "I never want to see my Dad again."

In December 1983, David left the hospital. When David returned to school, classmates welcomed him like a celebrity.

In 1984 Marie and David moved to California to be near plastic surgeon Dr. Bruce Achauer. In all, David had over 100 skin grafts.

David also suffered casual cruelty when people exclaimed, "Did you see that?" or "What an ugly kid!" Marie tried to instill a sense of purpose in her son, telling him he can "show people how to accept each other for what they have on the inside."

Despite the trauma and physical scars, David appeared psychologically healthy as he grew into adolescence. Nevertheless, Marie had psychiatrists regularly examine him, noting, "You never know what could be brewing inside."

Charles was paroled in January 1990. Nancy Wride wrote in the *Los Angeles Times*, "Because he was largely a model prisoner, state law allowed him a day off his sentence for every day he worked behind bars." He was placed under tough parole restrictions: an electronic monitor, 24-hour surveillance, and even a parole agent living with him.

David, then 13, was fearful and slept with a BB gun nearby. "I'd shoot his eye out if he ever came over," David said. "I'd blind him." Marie affectionately called David a "disgustingly normal" teenager who enjoyed sports and art and "wants to wear a tux and ride a limo to the school dance."

In 1993, Charles appeared on *Larry King Live*. King asked, "Why, Charles, did you decide to come forward and talk about this tonight?"

Charles answered, "My son has been exploited for the last ten years ... by many of the press and I'm tired of it. And it also puts me in a position where I'm being exploited."

Later Charles said, "The media, as you know, Larry, they're only interested in ratings and money. They don't care about my son. And they don't care about me; they don't care about his mother. A lot of talk shows—I want to exclude you, Oprah Winfrey, Koppel, and Barbara Walters—they're only interested in ratings."

Columnist Mike Royko wrote that after Charles "turned into a TV critic," Royko phoned the show to talk to Charles but "couldn't get through and in a few minutes the show ended."

He intended to tell Charles, "Your ex-wife fears you and your mutilated son fears you ... You should do the right thing ... get a bucket of kerosene, pour it on your head and light up. Do that and I assure you that many of us in the media will have nothing but kind words for you. Such as: 'Way to go, Charlie.'" Royko continued, "So maybe Charlie will read this. And if you do, Charlie, you don't have to bother with the kerosene. A high bridge or rooftop will do."

In January 1996, police arrested Charles, charging him with shooting and killing another ex-convict. David decided to confront the man who had caused him so much agony. Charles wrote in a letter to the *Los Angeles Times* that he wanted to see David and accept responsibility for harming him.

Protective glass blocked them from physical contact during the jailhouse visit. David recalled, "It was something I've always dreaded but I knew the time had come for me to confront him and get him out of my life once and for all. I was nervous but the moment I saw him I just ripped him to shreds ... I beat him up verbally. He had the nerve to keep telling me he loved me. I screamed at him, 'Look at me! You don't love me, you lying son of a bitch!' In thirty minutes, I got fourteen years of bottled up emotions off my chest ... He was shaking as I yelled at him. Was he upset? I damn well hope so. I walked into that jail all stressed out but as I left I realized a great weight had been lifted from my shoulders." David elaborated,

"I'm getting on with my life and I never need to see that bastard father of mine ever again."

Charles was cleared of the charges connected with the shooting and released.

Since reaching adulthood, David has played the role of a burn victim in the soap opera The Bold and the Beautiful and directed music videos. Kevin O'Sullivan wrote in a British magazine called The People, "[David] drives a Honda Civic, regularly jogs three miles, and shares his Los Angeles apartment with his pet dog Josephine." It is difficult for him to tie his shoelaces and button his clothes because his fingers are fused but he does those things. "I am my own man," David said. "I make my own decisions—I am not an invalid." He has shed the name Rothenberg and calls himself "Dave Dave."

In 2005, Charles, having legally changed his name to Charley Charles, was charged with being a felon in possession of a handgun. Under California's "three strikes" law, he was sentenced to life imprisonment. The sentence allows for the possibility of parole but it seems improbable a parole board will ever release this notorious habitual offender. Rather, it is likely he will end his life as he has spent so much of it: a pariah even among prison inmates, a man despised, lonely, isolated, and incarcerated.

Bibliography

"Dave Rothenberg, David Rothenberg Burn Victim, Charles Rothenberg."http://davidrothenbergmovie.blogspot. com/2011/02/dave-rothenberg-david-rothenberg-burn.html. Feb. 8, 2011.

"Dave   Dave."   https://www.facebook.com/pages/Dave-Dave/177068897746.

"David Rothenberg – Burn Victim (Dave Dave)." http://mich-ipato.wordpress.com/2010/05/02/david-rothenberg-burn-victim-dave-dave. January 2013.

"David Rothenberg Meets Jailed Father." *Los Angeles Times*. June 8, 1996.

Fried, Joseph P. "Man Who Set Son Afire Faces New Arson Trial." *The New York Times*. June 9, 2002.

Gaynor, Harry J.; Wilson, Jack; and Savicky, Andrew. *A World Without Tears: The Case of Charles Rothenberg*. Praeger Publishers. 1990.

"Man who burned his son sentenced in gun case." **Los Angeles Times.** April 5, 2007.

O'Sullivan, Kevin. "David's dad set him on fire and left him to die … today he's a young man in love!" *The People*. The Free Library.com. December 22, 1996.

Romney, Lee. "A Reviled Criminal Faces a Third Strike." *Los Angeles Times*. Jan. 26, 2005.

Rothenberg, Marie and White, Mel. David. *Guideposts*. 1985.

Rothenberg, Marie. "Three Years After His Father Set Him Afire, David Rothenberg Not Only Survives but Smiles." *People*. June 9, 1986.

Royko, Mike. "Larry King's Talk Show Offers A Gall-star Guest." Tribune Media Services. *Orlando Sentinel*. Oct. 6, 1993.

"Tragic Burns Boy Hits Hollywood Big Time!" http://www.thefreelibrary.com/TRAGIC+BURNS+BOY+HITS+HOLLYWOOD+BIG+TIME!-a061113474.

Wride, Nancy. "Burn Victim Dreads Day His Father Gets Paroled." *Los Angeles Times*. Jan. 21, 1990.